Student Book

ignite
English

Geoff Barton

Jill Carter

Peter Ellison

Liz Hanton

Mel Peeling

Alison Smith

Consultant

Geoff Barton

OXFORD
UNIVERSITY PRESS

OXFORD
UNIVERSITY PRESS

Great Clarendon Street, Oxford, OX2 6DP, United Kingdom

Oxford University Press is a department of the University of Oxford. It furthers the University's objective of excellence in research, scholarship, and education by publishing worldwide. Oxford is a registered trade mark of Oxford University Press in the UK and in certain other countries

© Oxford University Press 2014

First published in 2014

All rights reserved. No part of this publication may be reproduced, stored in a retrieval system, or transmitted, in any form or by any means, without the prior permission in writing of Oxford University Press, or as expressly permitted by law, by licence or under terms agreed with the appropriate reprographics rights organization. Enquiries concerning reproduction outside the scope of the above should be sent to the Rights Department, Oxford University Press, at the address above.

You must not circulate this work in any other form and you must impose this same condition on any acquirer

British Library Cataloguing in Publication Data

Data available

978-0-19-839244-6

10 9 8

Paper used in the production of this book is a natural, recyclable product made from wood grown in sustainable forests. The manufacturing process conforms to the environmental regulations of the country of origin.

Printed in India by Multivista Global Pvt. Ltd

Acknowledgements

The publishers would like to thank the following for permissions to use their photographs:

Cover: The Print Collector/Alamy; Paddington/Shutterstock; Nicole Gordine/Shutterstock; lavitrei/Shutterstock; Ekaterina Prilipova/Shutterstock; Longjourneys/Shutterstock; jl661227/Shutterstock; Creativa/Shutterstock; Ideas_ supermarket/Shutterstock; **p8-9:** Piotr Krzeslak/Shutterstock; **p8:** pockygallery/Shutterstock; **p9:** Ivancovlad/ Shutterstock; **p10-11**: Late Night Rabbit/Shutterstock; **p11:** Silm/Shutterstock; **p12-13:** Joyce Vincent/Shutterstock; **p12:** Orfeev/Shutterstock; **p14-15:** Longjourneys/Shutterstock; **p14-15:** Migogo/Shutterstock; **p14-15:** Shukaylova Zinaida/ shutterstock; **p14:** VectorShots/Shutterstock; **p15:** nikoniano/Shutterstock; **p16-17:** COTTCHA/shutterstock; **p16-17:** M2 Photography / Alamy; **p16-17:** s_oleg/Shutterstock; **p17:** AF archive/Alamy; **p18-19:** james weston/Shutterstock; **p18-19:** Szantai Istvan/Shutterstock; **p19:** Hein Nouwens/Shutterstock; **p20:** imagebroker/Alamy; **p21:** Makc/Shutterstock; **p21:** Voropaev Vasiliy/Shutterstock; **p22:** pockygallery/Shutterstock; **p24-25:** Jamen Percy/Shutterstock; **p24-25:** jgl247/ shutterstock; **p24-25:** jgl247/shutterstock; p24-25: Maglara/Shutterstock; p24-25: PRILL/Shutterstock; p24-25: Reinhold Leitner/Shutterstock; p24-25: Vitaly Korovin/Shutterstock; **p24:** Manuel Harlan; **p24:** The House of NyghtFalcon; **p26-27:** SergeyIT/Shutterstock; **p28-29:** Migogo/Shutterstock; **p31:** jgl247/shutterstock; **p32:** Mrs_ya/Shutterstock; **p32:** Nicole Gordine/Shutterstock; **p32:** risteski goce/Shutterstock; **p32:** Alexander Raths/shutterstock; **p32:** Andy Dean Photography/Shutterstock; **p32:** Atlaspix/Shutterstock; **p32:** auremar/shutterstock; **p32:** Dimedrol68/Shutterstock; **p32:** Matthew Dixon/Shutterstock; **p32:** Monkey Business Images/Shutterstock; **p32:** Nikos Psychogios/Shutterstock; **p32:** OLJ Studio/shutterstock; **p32:** Rich Carey/Shuttersock; **p32:** WDG Photo/Shutterstock; **p34:** visionaryft/Shutterstock; **p34:** ZUMA Press, Inc./Alamy; **p36-37:** Ansis Klucis/Shutterstock; **p37:** tratong/Shutterstock; **p37:** YuliaPodlesnova/ Shutterstock; **p38-39:** Africa Studio/Shutterstock; **p38-39:** Atlaspix/Shutterstock; **p39:** Feng Yu/Shutterstock; **p39:** Image Source/Alamy; **p40:** INTERFOTO / Alamy; **p40:** Ivan Vdovin/Alamy; **p40:** Radharc Images/Alamy; **p41:** Dimedrol68/ Shutterstock; **p42-43:** Antonio Abrignani/Shutterstock; **p42-43:** H1nksy/Shutterstock; **p43:** Roman Gorielov/ Shutterstock; **p44-45:** Chrupka/Shutterstock; **p44-45:** Lukiyanova Natalia/frenta/Shutterstock; **p44-45:** Pontus Edenberg/ Shutterstock; **p44:** Hung Chung Chih/Shutterstock; **p45:** astudio/Shutterstock; **p45:** Atiketta Sangasaeng/Shutterstock; **p45:** hvoya/Shutterstock; **p45:** ilmlandscape/Shutterstock; **p45:** Jacqui Martin/Shutterstock; **p45:** Silhouette Lover/ Shutterstock; **p45:** vdLee/Shutterstock; **p46-47:** nikit_a/Shutterstock; **p46-47:** EsbenOxholm/Shutterstock; **p47:** Tanchic/Shutterstock; **p48-49:** n_fransua/Shutterstock; **p48:** Africa Studio/Shutterstock; **p48:** Inga Dudkina/ Shutterstock; **p48:** Nicole Gordine/Shutterstock; **p49:** FXQuadro/Shutterstock; **p50:** PRISMA ARCHIVO/Alamy; **p50:** Sanjay Deva/Shutterstock; **p51:** Heritage Image Partnership Ltd/Alamy; **p51:** The art archive/Alamy; **p52-53:** Treenoot/ Shutterstock; **p52-53:** BrAt82/Shutterstock; **p52-53:** idea for life/Shutterstock; **p52-53:** Vladimir Tronin/Shutterstock; **p54-55:** Treenoot/Shutterstock; **p54-55:** Africa Studio/Shutterstock; **p54-55:** Oliver Hoffmann/Shutterstock; **p55:** aslysun/Shutterstock; **p58-59:** dacascas/Shutterstock; **p58-59:** Matthew Chattle/Alamy; **p58-59:** Nic Hamilton/Alamy; **p58-59:** Paprikubani; **p58-59:** Potapov Alexander; **p59:** Nic Hamilton Photographic/Alamy; **p60-61:** Africa Studio/ Shutterstock; **p60-61:** jannoon028/Shutterstock; **p61:** Digital Media Pro; **p61:** Eric Cote/Shutterstock; **p61:** JordiDelgado/ Shutterstock; **p61:** Julia Ivantsova/Shutterstock; **p61:** Rtimages/Shutterstock; **p64-65:** Maridav/Shutterstock; **p64:** oksana2010 /Shutterstock; **p65:** With kind permission from Mainstream Publishing/Random House; **p68-69:** momanuma/Shutterstock; **p68-69:** Volodymyr Goinyk/Shutterstock; **p71:** pockygallery/Shutterstock; **p70-71:** Andrew Zarivny/Shutterstock; **p70-71:** Banana Republic images/Shutterstock; p72-73: Hulton Archive/Getty images; p74: Ensuper/Shutterstock; p74: Picsfive/Shutterstock; **p74-75:** tommaso lizzulShutterstock; **p74:** freya-photographer/ Shutterstock; **p75:** Bobbie Osborne/Getty images; **p76-77:** James Osmond/Alamy; **p78-79:** Eduard Kyslynskyy/ Shutterstock; **p78-79:** saknakorn/Shutterstock; **p78-79:** Sergej Razvodovskij/Shutterstock; **p81:** Henning Riemer / Shutterstock; **p82-83:** enterlinedesign/Shutterstock; **p82:** dotshock/Shutterstock; **p82:** homydesign/Shutterstock; **p82:** tiptoee/Shutterstock; **p83:** Feng Yu/name tag/Shutterstock; **p83:** Mr Pics/Shutterstock; **p86-87:** Alef-Beth /Shutterstock; **p86-87:** gravity imaging /Shutterstock; **p86-87:** grynold/Shutterstock; **p86-87:** mskorpion/Shutterstock; **p86-87:** Nikiforov Volodymyr/Shutterstock; **p86-87:** Tom Burlison/Shutterstock; **p86:** Olegro/Shutterstock; **p88-89:** Brocreative/ Shutterstock; **p88-89:** goodgold99/Shutterstock; **p88:** Roman Gorielov/Shutterstock; **p88:** Roman Gorielov/Shutterstock; **p89:** Winston Link /Shutterstock; **p90-91:** ID1974/Shutterstock; **p90:** RAStudio/Shutterstock; **p90:** ZUMA Press, Inc./ Alamy; **p92:** Angela Hawkey/Shutterstock; **p92:** Anna Bryukhanova/Getty images; **p92:** Chris Rose/Alamy; **p92:** CREATISTA /iStock; **p93:** The Print Collector/Alamy; **p94-95:** redorbital./Demotix/Corbis; **p95:** dbimages/Alamy; **p96-97:** age fotostock/Alamy; **p98:** twitter Inc; **p99:** Facebook; **p99:** Instagram; **p99:** maximimages.com/Alamy; **p100:** Ian Dagnall/Alamy; **p101:** Tracksimages.com/Alamy; **p102-103:** dwphotos/Shutterstock; **p102:** Feng Yu/name tag/ Shutterstock; **p103:** Mr Pics/Shutterstock; **p104-105:** fotomak/Shutterstock; **p104-105:** Natursports/Shutterstock; **p104:** Dahabian/Shutterstock; **p104:** RAStudio/Shutterstock; **p105:** Franz Pfluegl; **p106-107:** Luciano Mortula/Shutterstock; **p106-107:** Marc Bruxelle/Shutterstock; **p106-107:** Kjpargeter/Shutterstock; **p106-107:** REX/Juha Sorri; **p106:** Atlaspix/ Shutterstock; **p106:** Chris Parypa Photography/Shutterstock; **p106:** Ivonne Wierink/Shutterstock; **p106:** REX/David Fisher; **p106:** Rune Hellestad/Corbis; **p106:** Thomas Skjaeveland/Shutterstock; **p108:** M&N/Alamy; **p108:** Olga Selyutina/ Shutterstock; **p110-111:** annoon028/Shutterstock; **p112-113:** melis/Shutterstock; **p113:** Featureflash/Shutterstock; **p113:** Featureflash/Shutterstock; **p114-115:** Antun Hirsman/Shutterstock; **p114-115:** cretolamna/Shutterstock; **p114-115:** leungchopan/Shutterstock; **p114:** Peshkova/Shutterstock; **p116:** Jagodka/Shutterstock; **p119:** AlamyCelebrity/Alamy; **p120-121:** Feng Yu/Shutterstock; **p120-121:** Reinhold Leitner/Shutterstock; **p122:** Jeffrey Blackler / Alamy; p122: Stephen Finn / Alamy; p123: AlamyCelebrity / Alamy; p123: amenic181/Shutterstock; p124-125: AVAVA/Shutterstock; **p126-127:** BBC; **p126:** Rex; **p130-131:** sbko/Shutterstock; **p130:** sbko/Shutterstock; **p130:** takayuki/Shutterstock; **p131:** Bronwyn Photo/Shutterstock; **p134-135:** DavidPinoPhotography/Shutterstock; **p138-139:** Karel Gallas/Shutterstock; **p140:** Jill Battaglia/Shutterstock; **p140:** Jill Battaglia/Shutterstock; **p140:** Jill Battaglia/ Shutterstock; **p140:** Lebrecht Music and Arts Photo Library/Alamy; **p140:** Vittorio Bruno/Shutterstock; **p142-143:** bomg/Shutterstock; **p142-143:** bomg/Shutterstock; **p142-143:** bomg/Shutterstock; **p142:** Oxford University Press; **p143:** Classic Image/Alamy; **p143:** North Wind Picture Archives/Alamy; **p144-145:** maigi/Shutterstock; **p144:** iofoto/ Shutterstock; **p144:** Crepesoles/Shutterstock; **p144:** kostudio/Shutterstock; **p144:** kungverylucky/Shutterstock; **p144:** Tanjala Gica/Shutterstock; **p144:** Yulia Mayorova/Shutterstock; **p145:** Mike Laptev/Shutterstock; **p145:** Ruth Black/Shutterstock; **p146-147:** 2happy/Shutterstock; **p146-147:** Aaron Amat/Shutterstock; **p146-147:** Christopher Ewing/Shutterstock; **p146-147:** Feng Yu/Shutterstock; **p146-147:** Vitaly Korovin/Shutterstock; **p147:** Montagu Images/Alamy; **p148:** rvlsoft/Shutterstock; p148: The Protected Art Archive/Alamy; **p149:** Elizabeta Lexa/Shutterstock; **149:** Everett Collection Historical/Alamy; **p150-151:** Alekcey/Shutterstock; **p150-151:** Aaron Amat/Shutterstock; **p150-151:** Alamy/Alamy; **p150-151:** Stuart C. Wilson/Getty images; **p152:** Lagui/Shutterstock; **p152:** Andy Lidstone; **p152:** Laborant/Shutterstock; **p153:** photobank.ch/Shutterstock; **p154:** Elena Elisseeva/Shutterstock; **p154:** Jeanette Dietl/Shutterstock; **p154:** Madarakis/Shutterstock; **p154:** rvlsoft/Shutterstock; **p156-157:** Jill Battaglia/Shutterstock;

All other images by New Future Graphic.

The authors and publisher are grateful for permission to reprint extracts from the following copyright material:

Fleur Adcock: 'For Heidi with Blue Hair' and 'For Meg' from *Poems 1955-2005* (Bloodaxe, 2005), reprinted by permission of Blooc Books.

Simon Armitage: lines from 'Mother, any distance greater than a single span' from *Book of Matches* (Faber, 2001), reprinted by permission of Faber & Faber Ltd.

Linda Banche: 'Macaroni! And I Don't Mean Pasta!', June 2010, blog posted at http://www.lindabanche.blogspot.com, reprinted permission of the author, www.lindabanche.com

Elizabeth Bowen: 'The Demon Lover' in *The Demon Lover and Other Stories* (Jonathan Cape, 1945), reprinted by permission of The Random House Publishing Group.

Richard Branson: *Losing my Virginity: The Autobiography* (Virgin Books/Ebury, 2009), reprinted by permission of The Random Hou Publishing Group.

Christy Brown: *My Left Foot* (Secker & Warburg, 1954/Minerva Vintage, 1990), reprinted by permission of The Random House Publishing Group.

James Caan: *How to Start Your Business in 7 Days: Turn Your Business Idea into a Life-Changing Success* (Portfolio Penguin, 2012, 2013), copyright © James Caan 2012, reprinted by permission of Penguin Books Ltd.

Jeremy Clarkson: *The World According to Clarkson* (Penguin, 2005), copyright © Jeremy Clarkson 2004, reprinted by permission o Penguin Books Ltd.

Gillian Cross: *The Demon Headmaster* (OUP, 2004), copyright © Gillian Cross 1982, reprinted by permission of Oxford University

Caroline Davies and Ben Quinn: 'Duchess of Cambridge gives birth to baby boy, third in line to the throne', *The Guardian*, 22.7.2013, copyright © Guardian News and Media 2013, reprinted by permission of GNM Ltd.

Steve Doughty: 'How mobiles have created a generation without manners', *Daily Mail*, 5.9.2013, reprinted by permission of Sol Syndication.

Daphne du Maurier: 'The Birds', first published in *The Apple Tree* (Victor Gollancz, 1952) copyright © the Estate of Daphne du Maurier 1952, reprinted by permission of Curtis Brown Group Ltd, London, on behalf of The Chichester Partnership.

Kitty Empire: review of Emeli Sande, *The Observer*, 14.4.2013, copyright © Guardian News and Media 2013, reprinted by permis of GNM Ltd.

John Friedman: 'You are what you Tweet: how social media define our professional brands' *Huffington Post*, 11 May 2012, reprir by permission of the author.

Robert Frost: 'A Time to Talk' from *Collected Poems* (Vintage Classics 2013), reprinted by permission of The Random House Publi Group.

Chrissie Gittins: 'Three' from I *Don't Want an Avocado for an Uncle* (Rabbit Hole, 2006), copyright © Chrissie Gittins 2006, reprint permission of the author.

James Gleick: *The Information: a history, a theory, a flood,* (Fourth Estate, 2011), copyright © James Gleick 2011, reprinted by permi of HarperCollins Publishers Ltd.

William Golding: *Lord of the Flies* (Faber, 1954), reprinted by permission of Faber & Faber Ltd.

Carrie Green: extract from an interview with Kanya King, *(This Girl Means) Business*, December 2012, reprinted by permission of author, www.FemaleEntrepreneurAssociation.com.

Adrian Henri: 'Without You', and lines from 'Love is...' from *The Mersey Sound* (Penguin, 2007), copyright © Adrian Henri 1967, reprinted by permission of The Estate of Adrian Henri c/o Rogers Coleridge & White Ltd, 20 Powis Mews, London W11 1JN.

Charlie Higson: *The Dead* (Puffin, 2010), copyright © Charlie Higson 2010, reprinted by permission of Penguin Books Ltd.

Susan Hill: *The Woman in Black* (Vintage, 1998), copyright © Susan Hill 1983, reprinted by permission of Sheil Land Associates Lt

Jenny Joseph: 'Warning' from *Selected Poems* (Bloodaxe, 1992), copyright © Jenny Joseph 1992, reprinted by permission of Johns Alcock Ltd for the author.

Liz Lochhead: 'Rapunzstiltskin' from *Dreaming Frankenstein* (Polygon, 2003), reprinted by permission of Polygon, an imprint of Birlinn Ltd (www.birlinn.co.uk).

Nick McDermott: 'Pushy Parents, Chasing Lost Dreams', *Daily Mail*, 20.6.2013, reprinted by permission of Solo Syndication.

Isaac Marion: *Warm Bodies* (Vintage, 2010), reprinted by permission of The Random House Group Ltd.

Sam Marsden and Andrew Hough: 'Children shouldn't have best friends, private school head argues', *The Telegraph*, 1.5.2013, copyright © Telegraph Media Group Ltd 2013, reprinted by permission of TMG Ltd.

Bryony Moore: 'Primark and the high street: Why are workers who make our cheap clothes paying with their lives?', *The Independent*, 26.4.2013, copyright © The Independent 2013, reprinted by permission of The Independent.

Patrick Ness: *The Knife of Never Letting Go* (Walker Books, 2013), copyright © Patrick Ness 2008, reprinted by permission of Walk Books Ltd, London SE11 5HJ, www.walker.co.uk

Tina Nielsen: 'Kanya King', *Director Magazine*, January 2010, reprinted by permission of The Institute of Directors.

Timothy Pallett, Miranda Hamilton and Chloe Hamilton: 'The digital etiquette generation game; is texting rude? Is voice for dinosaurs? And how should you sign off an email?', *The Independent*, 15.3.2013, copyright © The Independent 2013, reprinted permission of The Independent.

Sylvia Plath: 'You're' from *Collected Poems* (Faber, 2002), reprinted by permission of Faber & Faber Ltd.

Sarah Pinborough: *Mayhem* (Jo Fletcher, 2013), reprinted by permission of David Higham Associates Ltd.

Levi Roots: *You Can Get It If You Really Want* (Mitchell Beazley, 2011), copyright © Levi Roots 2011, reprinted by permission of The Octopus Publishing Group.

Danny Santiago (Daniel Lewis James): 'The Somebody', copyright © Danny Santiago 1970, first published in *Redbook Magazin* reprinted by permission of Brandt and Hochman Literary Agents, Inc. All rights reserved.

Anita Singh: 'Controversial Statue of Disabled Alison Unveiled' 15.9.2005, copyright © Press Association 2005, reprinted by permission of the Press Association.

Dan Travis: 'A Manifesto for the Reintroduction of Competition in Schools', reprinted by permission of the Manifesto Club, ww manifestoclub.com.

H G Wells: 'The Red Room' from *Complete Short Stories* (Ernest Benn, 1966), reprinted by permission of United Agents on behalf The Literary Executors of the Estate of H G Wells

and to the following for their permission to reprint extracts from copyright material:

Brandpie: for statement from www.brandpie.com

Guardian News and Media Limited for extract from an Interview with Charlie Higson, *The Guardian*, 24.9.2012, copyright © Guardian News and Media 2012; 'A Letter to my beautiful blue-eyed boy', *The Guardian*, 20.3.2012, copyright © Guardian News ar Media 2012; and 'Royal baby: Duchess of Cambridge gives birth to a boy - as it happened, live blog, theguardain.com, 22.7.2013, copyright © Guardian News and Media 2013.

HarperCollins Publishers Ltd for Dragons' Den: *The Perfect Pitch: How to Win Over an Audience* (HarperCollins, 2010), copyright HarperCollins Publishers 2010, Foreward copyright © Evan Davis 2010; and Dragons' Den: *Success from Pitch to Profit* (HarperColli 2008), copyright © HarperCollins Publishers 2007, Foreward, Epilogue and Part 3 copyright © Evan Davis 2007.

Interbrand for extract from Interbrand's *Best Global Brands in 2013* report published at http://www.interbrandfilehosting.com/ Interbrand-Best-Global-Brands-2013-Report.pdf

Oxford University Press for extract from Oxford Words Blog: 'Buzzworthy words added to Oxford Dictionaries online - Squee! 28.8.2013, http://blog.oxforddictionaries.com

Reigate & Banstead Borough Council for extract from the 'Young People' report, Local Community Action Plan, Netherne-o the-Hill.

Richmond Council for extract from Press release (July 2012) www.richmond.gov.uk.

John Wiley & Sons, Inc for extract from Dummies.com article 'Improving your inflection of the phone', copyright © dummies

Although we have made every effort to trace and contact all copyright holders before publication this has not been possible in cases. If notified, the publisher will rectify any errors or omissions at the earliest opportunity.

Links to third party websites are provided by Oxford in good faith and for information only. Oxford disclaims any responsibility for the materials contained in any third party website referenced in this work.

Ignite English has been written by people who love teaching English. It was a pre-requisite for us when developing this resource that you have people who are confident teaching English and who would find it patronizing to tell you how to teach English. Therefore we have provided a flexibility, both digitally and on the page, so that you can decide how you are going to customize it for your students.

In *Ignite English*, we also take English and show how it relates to the real world. Outside school there are lots of people doing lots of different jobs who will be using speaking, listening, reading and writing and we might not even think about how they are doing it. Well let's! In *Ignite English*, we take a look at what they do and we talk to them about how they are doing it, so that you and your students can explore the way they are using language and connect what we are doing in the classroom with the world out there.

Informed by research and recent Ofsted reports, *Ignite English* aims to help reinvigorate KS3 English teaching and learning by:

- Improving learning through relevance and creativity

- Ensuring teaching is distinctive

- Enabling effective transition between Year 6 and Year 7

- Accessing up-to-date and relevant professional development

- Delivering the new KS3 National Curriculum

That is essentially what we are trying to do with *Ignite English*.

Geoff Barton

Series Consultant, Head Teacher, Teacher of English and highly experienced English author

Ignite English authors

Ignite English was created with Geoff Barton and authored by experienced teachers and educationalists who are passionate about teaching English. As well as being tested in schools and reviewed by teachers, the resources were also reviewed by Peter Ellison, a cross-phase Local Authority Adviser and Phil Jarrett, former Ofsted National Adviser for English.

Contents

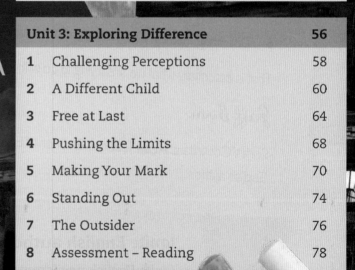

Overview of Ignite English

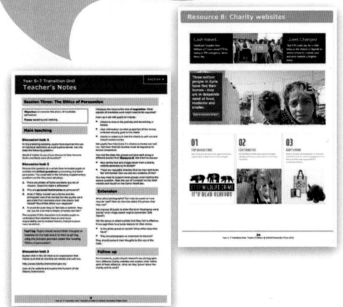

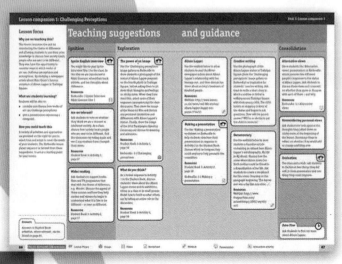

Transition support

Teacher Companion 1 includes English lesson suggestions and guidance on effective transition from Primary to Secondary school. It also includes a range of teaching ideas for the first week of English lessons in Secondary schools, with an opening lesson included in Student Book 1. In addition, there is a professional development unit specifically on transition in Kerboodle: Lessons, Resources and Assessments.

Also on Kerboodle LRA 1 and on the Oxford University Press *Ignite English* webpage, you will find a unit of work, with transition tips, for Primary school teachers to use in the final term of Year 6. This unit, 'Making a Difference', has *Ignite English* principles at its heart and we hope that by passing this unit on to local Primary schools it will foster enhanced relationships between Secondary school English departments and colleagues in local Primary schools.

Student Books

The Student Books have been designed to develop a range of reading, writing and spoken English skills in real-life contexts. Each Student Book offers thematically-focused units, covering prose fiction, poetry, drama and non-fiction forms, as well as a focus on language and one unique immersive unit based around a real-world scenario. They also feature an explicit focus on spelling, punctuation and grammar (SPAG). There is a wide range of source texts and activities with Stretch and Support as well as regular Progress Checks and Extra Time features, which can be used either for extension or homework.

Teacher Companions

Each Teacher Companion shares the thinking and philosophy behind the resources with a focus on the 'why', 'what' and 'how' of each unit, lesson and assessment. Additionally, the Teacher Companions feature unit-by-unit teaching support materials with comprehensive teaching tips, links and further reading suggestions. Each lesson features a Lesson Companion that includes a range of teaching ideas, guidance and tips to enable you to customize your lessons. The Teacher Companion also includes guidance and suggestions on setting up and marking the end of unit assessments.

Kerboodle: Lessons, Resources and Assessment

Kerboodle is packed full of guided support and ideas for creating and running effective lessons. It's intuitive to use, customizable, and can be accessed online anytime and anywhere. *Ignite English* Kerboodle LRA includes:

- 18 exclusive interviews providing over 40 unique and compelling films, connecting the learning in KS3 English lessons to skills used in thematically-linked jobs

- eight specially-commissioned filmed units providing CPD for English departments on key areas of Key Stage 3 teaching and learning, including genuine lesson footage, interviews with Primary and Secondary school teachers and students, and comments and observations from Geoff Barton and Phil Jarrett

- materials to support the transition for students from Key Stage 2 to Key Stage 3

- grammar support for teachers and students through extensive technical accuracy interactives and a grammar reference guide

- a wealth of additional resources including: interactive activities, an editable alternative end-of-unit assessment for every Student Book unit, marking scales to help monitor progress, photos, editable presentations, editable worksheets (general, differentiation and peer/self-assessment) and weblinks

- Lesson Player, enabling teachers to deliver ready-made lessons or the freedom to customize plans to suit your classes' needs.

Sarah Pinborough, Horror writer: Horror is a feeling.

Kerboodle Online Student Books

All three student books are also available as Online Student Books. These can be accessed on a range of devices, such as tablets, and offer a bank of tools to enable students to personalize their book and view notes left by the teacher.

DARE TO SCARE

How do horror stories scare us?

Introduction

Tales of terror have been sending shivers down readers' spines for centuries. Whether it's a ghost story read aloud on a dark stormy night, or vampires swooping across a cinema screen, there's something about horror which keeps us coming back for more.

In this unit, you will explore how writers of horror stories exploit our greatest fears, dare us to confront them, and take our imaginations on a rollercoaster ride of thrills and terror. You will be let into the secrets of creating the 'language of fear' so you too can lead your reader into the darkest recesses of their minds...

ignite INTERVIEW
Sarah Pinborough, Horror writer

To make a really effective horror story it should be a **metaphor** for something else that is happening in your main character's life. Get into your character's thoughts and feelings, because if we don't care about the character, we don't care if the monster eats him. With anything in a scary story, always think: 'less is more'. This means don't go over the top. Don't blood splatter. It is better to have sound effects, creepiness, someone becoming slightly disturbed by what they are hearing and build it up and build it up and build it up. Horror is a feeling.

✎ Activities

1a We all have a different fear threshold and are afraid of different things. List the three things that scare you the most. Compare your list with a partner's and agree which would be most likely to feature in a horror story and why.

1b Why do people enjoy being frightened by what they read? Join with another pair to share and agree on your top three reasons.

📖 Glossary

metaphor describing something as something else, not meant to be taken literally, e.g. *You are a star.*

1 Sinister Settings

↻ Objective

Analyse the themes and motifs of typical horror stories.

Common reoccurring images, sometimes called motifs, feature in many horror stories, because they help to create a mood of threat or fear.

✎ Activities

1a Look at the picture on this page and pick out some motifs that you might expect to find in a horror story. Complete a spider diagram, like the one started below, to note how each feature creates a feeling of fear or danger.

1b Discuss which motifs you think are the most frightening. Rank the top three scariest. Be prepared to explain your answers.

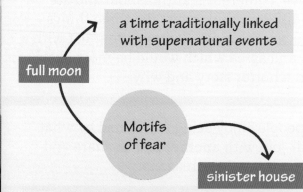

a time traditionally linked with supernatural events

full moon

Motifs of fear

sinister house

↔ Stretch

Add other motifs to your spider diagram that could be used in horror stories and explain how they are associated with fear and threat.

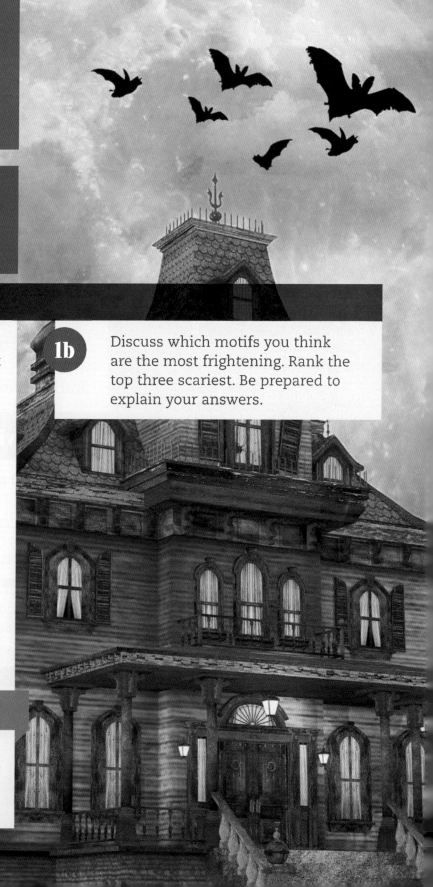

The extract below is taken from a short story called 'The Red Room' by H. G. Wells. Here, the narrator makes his way towards the room with the intention of spending the night there. He does so with trepidation because he has been told that a recent visitor died a mysterious death.

Extract from 'The Red Room' by H. G. Wells

The effect was scarcely what I expected, for the moonlight, coming in by the great window on the grand staircase, picked out everything in vivid black shadow or **reticulated** silvery illumination. Everything seemed in its proper position; the house might have been deserted on the yesterday instead of twelve months ago. There were candles in the sockets of the **sconces**, and whatever dust had gathered on the carpets or upon the polished flooring was distributed so evenly as to be invisible in my candlelight. A waiting stillness was over everything. I was about to advance, and stopped abruptly. A **bronze group** stood upon the landing hidden from me by a corner of the wall; but its shadow fell with marvelous distinctness upon the white paneling, and gave me the impression of some one crouching to **waylay** me... I stood rigid for half a moment perhaps…

The door of the Red Room and the steps up to it were in a shadowy corner. I moved my candle from side to side in order to see clearly the nature of the recess in which I stood, before opening the door. Here it was, thought I, that my predecessor was found, and the memory of that story gave me a sudden twinge of apprehension. I glanced over my shoulder… in the moonlight, and opened the door of the Red Room rather hastily, with my face half turned to the **pallid** silence of the corridor.

2 The use of certain colours can help to create a feeling of fear. List the colours mentioned in the **extract**. Explain how each one adds to the threatening atmosphere.

3 How else does the writer create a feeling of fear? Select some quotations and explain their effects.

📑 Support

Look for:

- horror motifs
- images that suggest the narrator is not alone
- descriptions of light, dark and shadows
- the narrator's reactions.

What do these tell us?

📖 Glossary

reticulated   net-like pattern

sconces   candle-holders fixed to walls

bronze group   bronze statue of a group of figures or animals

waylay   to unexpectedly interrupt or attack

pallid   pale

🕐 Extra Time

Write the next few paragraphs of 'The Red Room', continuing on from the end of the extract on this page. Try to maintain the style of the story.

2 From the Ordinary to the Extraordinary

↻ Objective

Analyse in detail how language can create atmosphere and build tension.

ignite INTERVIEW

'Atmosphere is key and it is all in your description.'

Sarah Pinborough

✎ Activities

1a The nouns and adjectives listed below are taken from the description of a house in a story. Looking at the words, what can you work out about the house?

SPAG

1b Using the words, create the most scary, chilling **noun phrases** you can by combining an adjective with a noun, e.g. steamy air. Explain how it might make a reader feel, e.g. *'Steamy air' creates a feeling of tension because it suggests hot and suffocating weather.*

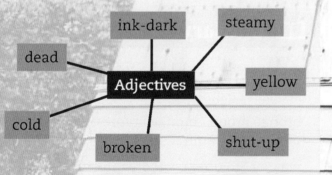

ink-dark   steamy
dead
Adjectives   yellow
cold
broken   shut-up

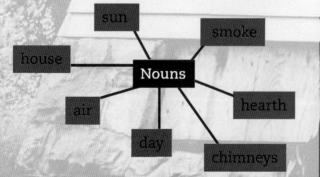

sun
smoke
house
Nouns
air   hearth
day
chimneys

📖 Glossary

noun phrase   a group of words built up around a single noun, e.g. *the very hungry snake.* The noun (*snake* in this example) is called the 'head' of the phrase because all the other words tell us something about the noun.

The adjectives and nouns in Activity 1a come from a description in a short story called 'The Demon Lover' written by Elizabeth Bowen. Read the extract from the story on the right and complete the activities below.

The story is set during the Second World War. At this point in the story, Mrs Drover returns to her boarded-up home.

2a How do the combinations of nouns and adjectives used by Elizabeth Bowen compare to the ones you created? Which do you think are the most effective and why? **SPAG**

2b Note the phrases from Bowen's description which create a sinister or **hostile** atmosphere. For each phrase, explain how the words are used to create this effect.

3 Using your notes and quotations from the text, write a paragraph to explain how the writer creates an atmosphere of tension.

📖 Glossary

hostile unfriendly; aggressive

silted up clogged up

warped bent or twisted out of shape

prosaic sensible

escritoire type of desk

parquet wooden floor

Extract from 'The Demon Lover' by Elizabeth Bowen

Toward the end of her day in London Mrs Drover went round to her shut-up house to look for several things she wanted to take away. Some belonged to herself, some to her family, who were by now used to their country life. It was late August; it had been a steamy, showery day. At the moment the trees down the pavement glittered in an escape of humid yellow afternoon sun. Against the next batch of clouds, already piling up ink-dark, broken chimneys and parapets stood out. In her once familiar street, as in any unused channel, an unfamiliar queerness had **silted up**; a cat wove itself in and out of railings, but no human eye watched Mrs Drover's return. Shifting some parcels under her arm, she slowly forced round her latchkey in an unwilling lock, then gave the door, which had **warped**, a push with her knee. Dead air came out to meet her as she went in.

The staircase window having been boarded up, no light came down into the hall. But one door, she could just see, stood ajar, so she went quickly through into the room and unshuttered the big window in there. Now the **prosaic** woman, looking about her, was more perplexed than she knew by everything that she saw, by traces of her long former habit of life – the yellow smoke stain up the white marble mantelpiece, the ring left by a vase on the top of the **escritoire**; the bruise in the wallpaper where, on the door being thrown open widely, the china handle had always hit the wall. The piano, having gone away to be stored, had left what looked like claw marks on its part of the **parquet**. Though not much dust had seeped in, each object wore a film of another kind; and, the only ventilation being the chimney, the whole drawing room smelled of the cold hearth.

3 You're Welcome...

↻ Objectives

- Use inference to explore characterization.

- Understand the use of irony.

Creating a character is a vital part of horror writing and the vampire is one of the stock characters of horror stories. Its popularity was given a huge boost in the 19th century by the publication in 1897 of *Dracula*, by Bram Stoker.

In the following extract, the novel's hero, Jonathan Harker, meets Count Dracula for the first time.

📖 Glossary

infer to work something out from what someone says or does, even though it is not directly stated

irony language that expresses the opposite of what is really meant

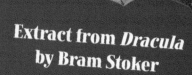

Extract from *Dracula* by Bram Stoker

I heard a heavy step approaching behind the great door, and saw through the chinks the gleam of a coming light. Then there was the sound of rattling chains and the clanking of massive bolts drawn back. A key was turned with the loud grating noise of long disuse, and the great door swung back.

Within, stood a tall old man, clean-shaven save for a long white moustache, and clad in black from head to foot, without a single speck of colour about him anywhere. He held in his hand an antique silver lamp, in which the flame burned without chimney or globe of any kind, throwing long, quivering shadows as it flickered in the draught of the open door. The old man motioned me in with his right hand with a courtly gesture, saying in excellent English, but with a strange intonation:–

'Welcome to my house! Enter freely and of your own free will!' He made no motion of stepping to meet me, but stood like a statue, as though his gesture of welcome had fixed him into stone. The instant, however, that I had stepped over the threshold, he moved impulsively forward, and holding out his hand grasped mine with a strength which made me wince, an effect which was not lessened by the fact that it seemed cold as ice – more like the hand of a dead than a living man.

✎ Activities

1a The writer gives clues that the Count is 'unusual'. Select some quotations that contain these clues and explain what the reader might **infer** from them. Record your ideas in a grid like the one started below.

Quotation	What I can infer from this
'Clad in black from head to foot, without a single speck of colour about him anywhere.'	The fact that he is dressed completely in black links him to night time and to darkness or evil.

1b The writer uses the adjective 'courtly' in this description. What does this mean and what associations does it have? Why is it a surprising word to describe a vampire's behaviour? **SPAG**

🗐 Support

Look up the word 'courtly' in a dictionary. Think about the wild, aggressive image of a vampire feeding on its prey. How does the adjective 'courtly' contrast with this?

2 The Count tells Harker that he is 'welcome'. There is some **irony** in this statement. Explain what the Count *appears* to mean and what the reader suspects that the Count *really* means.

3 How does the writer build up our impression of the Count in this description? Look closely at the structure of the paragraphs and sentences. How do they create a feeling of unease? **SPAG**

4 Write the opening paragraphs of your own original horror story. Look back at Sarah Pinborough's characterization advice on page 9 before starting.

🕐 Extra Time

Finish writing your horror story. Read it through and edit it to make it more effective.

15

4 Attack!

↻ Objective

Comment on how writers use sentence structure, word choice and imagery to create impact and drama.

Some horror stories portray scenes of violent physical conflict. These often contain a nightmarish quality, whereby something that should be ordinary and harmless turns hostile and aggressive.

The extract on the right is from a short story called 'The Birds' by Daphne du Maurier. The hero, Nat, is forced to fight off an attack by a vicious and bloodthirsty flock of gulls.

✎ Activities

1a Choose four verbs from the extract that you feel are particularly powerful in creating a sense of drama, violence or terror. Explain why you think these verbs are effective.

SPAG

1b In moments of physical danger, our senses become heightened to help us survive. How does the author give this impression to the reader?

1c Why does Nat want to keep the birds away from his eyes? Why does the author choose not to explain Nat's fears fully, allowing readers to draw their own conclusions and imagine the consequences? Is this more or less scary than a full description?

Extract from 'The Birds' by Daphne du Maurier

Covering his head with his arms, he ran towards the cottage. They kept coming at him from the air, silent save for the beating wings. The terrible, fluttering wings. He could feel the blood on his hands, his wrists, his neck. Each stab of a swooping beak tore into his flesh. If only he could keep them from his eyes. Nothing else mattered. He must keep them from his eyes. They had not learnt yet how to cling to a shoulder, how to rip clothing, how to dive in mass upon the head, upon the body. But with each dive, with each attack, they became bolder. And they had no thought for themselves. When they dived low and missed, they crashed, bruised and broken, on the ground. As Nat ran he stumbled, kicking their spent bodies in front of him.

He found the door, he hammered upon it with his bleeding hands. Because of the boarded windows no light shone. Everything was dark.

'Let me in,' he shouted, 'it's Nat. Let me in.'

He shouted loud to make himself heard above the whir of the gulls' wings.

SPAG

2 How does the writer use different sentence structures and language patterns in the extract to help the reader feel Nat's terror? Complete a grid, like the one started below, to explain the effect of the writer's language.

Language feature	Quotations	Effect
Short, **simple sentence**		
Complex sentence, with a subordinate clause	'They kept coming at him from the air, silent save for the beating wings.'	
Repetition of words		
Repetition of phrases		*Shows Nat's desperation*
Patterns of three		

Alfred Hitchcock was a legendary film director, often referred to as the master of suspense and horror. He directed a film version of the story.

3 Look at the poster advertising the film. Which elements of the poster are designed to suggest fear? If you were to create a new poster for the film, what would you put on it and why?

📖 **Glossary**

simple sentence   sentence made up of a single main clause with one main verb, e.g. *The lady appeared in the mist.*

complex sentence   sentence made up of a main clause and at least one subordinate (dependent) clause. The subordinate clause usually adds extra information to the sentence, but doesn't make sense on its own, e.g. *The lady, who was dressed completely in black, appeared from the mist.*

"...and remember, the next scream you hear may be your own!"

ALFRED HITCHCOCK'S "The Birds"

TECHNICOLOR®

ROD TAYLOR · JESSICA TANDY
SUZANNE PLESHETTE *and Introducing* 'TIPPI' HEDREN

Based on Daphne Du Maurier's Classic Suspense Story!

A Fascinating New Personality

Screenplay by EVAN HUNTER · Directed by ALFRED HITCHCOCK

More to explore

The Demon Headmaster is a chilling horror story for children. Again, the author, Gillian Cross, uses the technique of turning a 'normal' setting into a nightmarish situation.

The extract below describes another attack scene. The heroine, Dinah, and a few of her friends are refusing to obey the Demon Head, who wants to hypnotize the entire country through the TV. The friends are cornered in the boiler room by the Head, who summons his army of hypnotized students to back him up.

Glossary

belligerently
aggressively, as if looking for a fight

simile a comparison that uses the words 'like' or 'as', e.g. *as white as snow*

Extract from *The Demon Headmaster* by Gillian Cross

'You cannot refuse to do what I want.'

'Can't I?' Dinah stepped forward **belligerently**, but the Headmaster did not look in the least worried. Turning to the children massed in the doorway, he snapped at them in a brisk voice.

'Listen to my orders. In front of you are six straw dolls. They are no longer needed. You will advance on them and,' he drew a deep breath, 'you will tear them to pieces.'

Simultaneously, all the children swivelled their eyes to look into the boiler room. They showed no signs of recognition. It was plain that they were seeing precisely what they had been told to see. As they started to advance, Dinah watched Lucy, who was in the middle of the front row. Her face was as calm and cheerful as if she had been going out to pick daisies.

Knowing it would be no use, Dinah began to yell at her as the children marched into the boiler room.

'Lucy! It's me, Dinah! And there's Lloyd and Harvey and the others. You can't hurt us!'

'She won't hear you,' the Headmaster said icily. 'She is programmed to listen only to me and the prefects.'

Dinah and the others cowered against the wall behind them as the children came steadily tramping towards them.

'Think, Dinah think!' Lloyd yelled. 'There must be some way out of this. Otherwise they'll kill us.'

The foremost children had reached them now. Slowly they raised their arms, hands outstretched like claws.

'Oh help!' Harvey yelled. 'Someone, help!'

The claw-like hands grabbed. Dinah found her blazer gripped firmly by Lucy and she heard Mandy's blouse rip. From beside her, Ingrid wailed…

More and more hands were pulling at them. Glancing across the room, Dinah saw the Headmaster smiling calmly, with no sign of wavering. Coldly, she realized that he would not relent. If he had to kill them, he would kill them.

Activities continued

4a Look again at the extract on page 16 and the extract from 'The Birds' on page 18. Compare the techniques that the authors use to create a sense of horror. Follow the steps below, noting similarities and differences. **SPAG**

Make notes on the language techniques used by the authors. For example: the use of repetition and the use of simple, compound or complex sentences.

Identify the imagery that each author uses and explain the associations it conveys. For example, what does the **simile** 'hands like claws' suggest to you?

Look carefully at each author's vocabulary, particularly at the verbs and adverbs. What effect do they create in the reader's mind?

'The Birds' was written for adults, while *The Demon Headmaster* was written for children. Does this affect the way the authors have used language in these extracts?

Stretch

Good writers use layering techniques to add detail and reinforce themes. In horror stories, this layering technique is often used to give the impression that the evil is unstoppable and relentless. Consider how either or both of the writers use this technique in these extracts.

4b Use your notes to write a short report, comparing how the authors use language techniques to build up a sense of horror in these extracts. While making comparisons you could use the following phrases:

- Both authors use…
- Whereas du Maurier uses…
- In comparison…
- Another technique that both authors use is…
- A similar example of…
- In contrast…

As you write, remember to:

- include quotations to back up your points
- make sure you explain the effects of the techniques, and do not just list them
- group your ideas together in paragraphs. Start a new paragraph for a different topic.

Progress Check

Swap your draft report with a partner's and give them a rating from 1–3 (3 being the highest) for each of the three bullet points listed above.

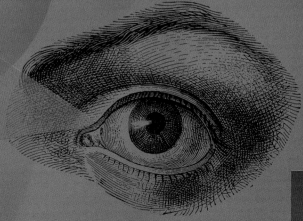

5 All in the Mind

↻ Objective

Explore a range of themes in psychological horror stories.

Horror comes in many forms. We can be horrified by violent physical confrontations or by blood and gore, or simply by ideas that prey on our minds and play with our deepest psychological fears, such as death, decay, loss and the supernatural.

✎ Activities

1 What do you think are our most deep-rooted fears in life? Here are some people's answers. Add at least two more.

I don't want to get old.

I'm afraid of being alone.

I think evil exists and it can control people and things.

2 Think about any frightening stories that you know (they might be films, stories, plays or poems). Explain what psychological fears they exploit and how they play upon the minds of the viewers or readers.

3 *The Strange Case of Dr Jekyll and Mr Hyde* is a classic horror story. What do you know about the story already? Read the blurb below, taken from the back of the novel. Then pick out the words or phrases that suggest that the novel is more of a psychological horror story. Explain your choices.

Dr Jekyll is obsessed by the idea of the soul's dual nature; he believes the good and evil sides of a person are distinct and can be separated, and seeks to prove this, despite the derision of his contempories.

Unpleasant Mr Hyde appears to be the perpetrator of a number of horrific and violent crimes, but when pursued by the police he is seemingly impossible to trace. Dr Jekyll appears to be his unlikely ally.

Lawyer, and concerned friend of Jekyll, Gabriel Utterson, takes it upon himself to investigate the strange happenings, though when the truth is finally revealed, it is far more sinister than anyone could have imagined…

The extract below is from Tennyson's poem 'Tithonus', in which a man regrets that the goddess, Eos, granted his wish for immortality.

Extract from 'Tithonus' by Afred Lord Tennyson

I ask'd thee, 'Give me immortality.'

Then didst **thou** grant mine asking with a smile,

Like wealthy men who care not how they give.

But thy strong Hours **indignant** work'd their wills,

And beat me down and **marr'd** and wasted me,

And tho' they could not end me, left me **maim'd**

To dwell in presence of immortal youth,

Immortal age beside immortal youth,

And all I was, in ashes. Can thy love,

Thy beauty, make amends, tho' even now,

Close over us, the silver star, thy guide,

Shines in those **tremulous** eyes that fill with tears

To hear me? Let me go; take back thy gift.

Why should a man desire in any way

To vary from the kindly race of men,

Or pass beyond the goal of **ordinance**

Where all should pause, as is most **meet** for all?

4a In your own words, explain the horror of the man's situation.

4c What is the moral (lesson about behaviour) that this poem gives the reader?

4b What words and images make you sympathize with the narrator of the poem?

 **Support**

Look in particular at the description given about the effect of 'Hours' (time) on the narrator.

Stretch

Look carefully at the two questions that the narrator asks. What does he beg the gods to do?

Glossary

thou   you

indignant   angry, often with a sense of injustice

marr'd   spoiled

maim'd   physically damaged or injured

tremulous   trembling

ordinance   what is decreed or ordered

meet   suitable

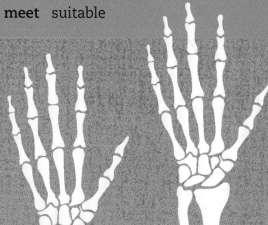

⑥ Graphic Detail

↻ Objective

Compare the effectiveness of graphic horror with psychological horror.

Do you enjoy reading about gross and gory things which turn other people's stomachs to jelly? Read on to explore how some writers choose to be very direct in their descriptions of horrific happenings in order to satisfy some readers' appetite for graphic horror.

In Charlie Higson's novel *The Dead*, a group of teenagers have to fight for survival in a world overrun by zombies. Look carefully at how the author creates horror in his description of a group of disease-ridden, zombie teachers.

Extract from *The Dead* by Charlie Higson

The teachers were advancing across the yard, and as they drew closer Ed got a good look at them. Their eyes were yellow and bulging, their skin lumpy with boils and growths, horrible pearly blisters nestling in folds. They were streaked with foam and one or two of them had bright red blood dribbling from their mouths. One had an ear hanging off. It flapped as he waddled along. Another had a sort of huge fleshy growth bulging out from his shirt, as if he'd swallowed a desk lamp. His whole body was twisted and misshapen.

✎ Activities

1a Write down the three most graphic quotations from the extract. What reaction do you think the writer is trying to trigger in the reader? Which image do you find most disturbing and why?

1b Write down any words or phrases from the extract which could be viewed as funny or comical. Explain why the writer may have mixed gory and amusing images.

1c Give reasons why the writer might have chosen to describe *teachers* in such a shocking and graphic way.

1d Create a spider diagram with suggestions for words and phrases that could be used to describe the zombie teachers in a way that is psychologically scary rather than graphic and shocking. Which form of horror do you prefer and why?

In an interview, Charlie Higson talks about why he writes about physical gore in some of his horror stories.

Zombie stories, like all the best horror stories, are about death and decay and disease and how horrible the insides of our bodies are. We don't want to think about all the yucky stuff squashed in there, our blood, our hearts, our livers and kidneys and lungs, most of all we don't want to think about our intestines… But zombie stories force us to think about these things, to confront our fears, in, I hope, an entertaining and thought-provoking way. Zombie stories remind us that we are all, in the end, just meat.

2a Write a paragraph in which you describe a zombie or monster. Make it a gory paragraph like the one by Charlie Higson and bear in mind what he says about 'confronting our fears'.

2b Write another paragraph in which you describe the creature in a less graphic but psychologically frightening way to prey on the reader's mind.

2c Swap your paragraphs with a partner. Read the new paragraphs and write a couple of sentences at the bottom of the work to explain which paragraph you find the most frightening and why.

ignite INTERVIEW

'Don't blood splatter, because where do you go from there? If you have got someone's guts all over the walls on page two, where can you take that story?'

Sarah Pinborough

🕐 Extra Time

Read the first of Charlie Higson's futuristic 'Enemy' series of novels. It's called *The Enemy* and is about a disease which turns adults into zombies.

7 The Supernatural on Stage

↺ Objective

Experiment with different techniques of conveying horror in a dramatic scene.

Supernatural elements have long been a feature of plays as well as novels and poems. In Shakespeare's *Macbeth*, the ghost of Banquo haunts King Macbeth, who is secretly responsible for his grisly murder.

✎ Activities

1a Look at the two photos below, taken from different performances of *Macbeth*. How do the images differ in terms of costume, setting, the way that Banquo is presented and the reactions of the other characters on stage?

1b Which approach do you think would convey the horror of the scene most effectively?

2 In groups, prepare a performance of the extract on page 25. Consider:

- how you will represent Banquo (Will he look ghostly/ordinary/shockingly gory/invisible?)

- how each character might be feeling

- how to convey each character's feelings through their expressions and movement

- how to vary pace, volume and tone to create maximum impact on the audience.

Extract from *Macbeth* by William Shakespeare

The GHOST OF BANQUO enters, and sits in MACBETH's place

Macbeth	Here had we now our country's honour roof'd, Were the graced person of our Banquo present; Who may I rather challenge for unkindness Than pity for **mischance**!
Ross	His absence, sir, Lays blame upon his promise. Please't your highness To grace us with your royal company.
Macbeth	The table's full.
Lennox	Here is a place reserved, sir.
Macbeth	Where?
Lennox	Here, my good lord. What is't that moves your highness?
Macbeth	Which of you have done this?
Lords	What, my good lord?
Macbeth	Thou canst not say I did it: never shake Thy gory locks at me.
Ross	Gentlemen, rise: his highness is not well.
Lady Macbeth	Sit, worthy friends: my lord is often thus, And hath been from his youth: pray you, keep seat; The fit is momentary; upon a thought He will again be well: if much you note him, You shall offend him and extend his passion: Feed, and regard him not. Are you a man?
Macbeth	Ay, and a bold one, that dare look on that Which might appal the devil.
Lady Macbeth	O proper stuff! This is the very painting of your fear: This is the air-drawn dagger which, you said, Led you to Duncan. O, these flaws and starts, Impostors to true fear, would well become A woman's story at a winter's fire, Authorized by her **grandam**. Shame itself! Why do you make such faces? When all's done, You look but on a stool.

📖 Glossary

mischance   bad luck
grandam   grandmother

☑ Progress Check

Perform your scene in front of other students. Ask them to give your group a rating on a scale of 1–3 (3 being the highest) on the following aspects:

- how well you used your voices to convey the terror and confusion felt by Macbeth and his courtiers
- how clearly your body language and facial expressions displayed a sense of drama
- how horrifically or hauntingly Banquo's ghost was portrayed.

RESERVED

8 Tenses and Tension

↻ Objective

Explore how verb tense influences the narrative voice and its effect on the reader.

As readers, we relish the thrill of being frightened. The more immediate the danger or horror seems to be, the more frightening it becomes.

The Knife of Never Letting Go by Patrick Ness is a novel written from the perspective of teenager, Todd, as he struggles to survive in a nightmarish futuristic world. In the extract on the right, Todd and his companion, Viola, are cornered in a church by Aaron, an evil priest.

Extract from *The Knife of Never Letting Go* by Patrick Ness

'Go!' I yell–

But she's got a big flat stone in her hands and launches it at Aaron with a grimace and an angry grunt and he ducks and tries to deflect it with one hand but it catches him cross the forehead, causing him to stumble away from both her and me, towards the ledge, towards the front of the church–

'Come on!" Viola yells to me–

I scramble to my feet–

But Aaron's turned, too–

Blood running down his face–

His mouth open in a yell–

He jumps forward like a spider, grabbing Viola's right arm–

She punches fiercely with her left hand, bloodying it on his face–

But he don't let go–

I'm yelling as I fly at them–

Knife out–

But again I turn at the last minute–

And I just knock into him–

We land on the upslope of the stairs, Viola falling back, me on top of Aaron, his arms boxing my head and he reaches forward with his horrible face and *takes a bite* out of an exposed area of my neck–

Activities

1 The writer uses a variety of techniques to make this scene tense and dramatic. Complete a spider diagram like the one started below. Give examples of the techniques used in the extract and explain the effect they have on the tension.

ignite INTERVIEW

'If it's a short story, only stay in one character's head. If you start jumping around with perspectives, you lose the focus.'

Sarah Pinborough

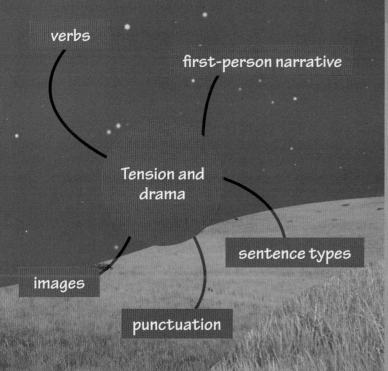

verbs

first-person narrative

Tension and drama

images

sentence types

punctuation

2a Most novels are written in the past tense, but this one is written in the present tense. Rewrite the extract in the past tense, starting:

SPAG

'Go!' I yelled.

But she had a big flat stone in her hands...

2b Which version do you think is the most dramatic – the original, present-tense version, or your own past-tense version? Give reasons for your answer.

☑ Progress Check

Write a paragraph to describe what you imagine happens next in the fight between Todd, Viola and Aaron. Write in the first person, using 'I', and in the present tense. Try to use some of the techniques Patrick Ness uses in order to make your own paragraph as dramatic as possible, e.g. powerful verbs, different sentence types and imagery.

SPAG

Swap your paragraph with a partner and give them a rating from 1–3 (3 being the best) for the following:

- how exciting their paragraph is
- the range of techniques used to increase the drama
- the believability of the narrative voice.

9 Assessment: Reading and Selecting Material for an Anthology

A publisher has asked for your help to compile a new anthology called *Tales of Terror to Terrify any Teen*. Your task is to read extracts from three horror stories on pages 29–31 and choose one to include in the anthology.

The publisher has asked you to present your findings as a report, giving a critical analysis of the extract that you are recommending. You will need to:

- suggest which text you think will have most appeal for a teenage audience and explain why
- include quotations from the text to support your ideas
- use Standard English and ensure that your report has an introduction, paragraphs that focus on different aspects or topics, and a conclusion.

Note that you are being tested on your reading skills, rather than your writing skills in this assessment.

Before you write…

Read all three extracts before making your choice. Think carefully about:

- the writer's depiction of setting, theme and characters
- the narrative viewpoint and use of verb tense
- the writer's language use (including sentence structure, word choice, imagery).

As you write…

Plan your report, making sure you group your ideas into a logical sequence of paragraphs. Write up your report.

When you have finished writing…

Present your report giving clear reasons for your recommendations.

Extract 1 from *Warm Bodies* by Isaac Marion

The city where we do our hunting is conveniently close. We arrive around noon the next day and start looking for flesh. The new hunger is a strange feeling. We don't feel it in our stomachs – some of us don't even have those. We feel it everywhere equally, a sinking, sagging sensation, as if our cells are deflating. Last winter, when so many Living joined the Dead and our prey became scarce, I watched some of my friends become full-dead. The **transition** was undramatic. They just slowed down, then stopped, and after a while I realised they were corpses. It disquieted me at first, but it's against **etiquette** to notice when one of us dies. I distracted myself with some groaning.

I think the world has mostly ended, because the cities we wander through are as rotten as we are. Buildings have collapsed. Rusted cars clog the streets. Most glass is shattered, and the wind drifting through the hollow high-rises moans like an animal left to die. I don't know what happened. Disease? War? Social collapse? Or was it just us? The Dead replacing the Living? I guess it's not so important. Once you've arrived at the end of the world, it hardly matters which route you took.

We start to smell the Living as we approach a dilapidated apartment building. The smell is not the musk of sweat and skin, but the **effervescence** of life energy, like the **ionised** tang of lightning and lavender. We don't smell it in our noses. It hits us deeper inside, near our brains, like **wasabi**. We converge on the building and crash our way inside.

We find them huddled in a small studio unit with the windows boarded up. They are dressed worse than we are, wrapped in filthy tatters and rags, all of them badly in need of a shave. M will be saddled with a short blond beard for the rest of his Fleshy existence, but everyone else in our party is clean-shaven. It's one of the perks of being Dead, another thing we don't have to worry about any more. Beards, hair, toenails … no more fighting biology. Our wild bodies have been finally tamed.

Slow and clumsy but with unswerving commitment, we launch ourselves at the Living. Shotgun blasts fill the dusty air with gunpowder and gore. Black blood spatters the walls. The loss of an arm, a leg, a portion of torso, this is disregarded, shrugged off. A minor **cosmetic** issue. But some of us take shots to our brains, and we drop. Apparently there's still something of value in that withered grey sponge, because if we lose it, we are corpses. The zombies to my left and right hit the ground with moist thuds. But there are plenty of us. We are overwhelming. We set upon the Living, and we eat.

📖 Glossary

transition change

etiquette rules of correct behaviour

effervescence fizz

ionised electrically charged

wasabi Japanese plant with strong-tasting root used in cookery

cosmetic superficial

More to explore

In this second extract a young lawyer, Arthur Kipps, is sent to sort out the affairs of an elderly lady who has died. At her funeral, Kipps encounters a mysterious woman.

Extract 2 from *The Woman in Black* by Susan Hill

…on hearing some slight rustle behind me, I half-turned, **discreetly**, and caught a glimpse of another **mourner**, a woman, who must have slipped into the church after we of the funeral party had taken our places and who stood several rows behind and quite alone, very erect and still, and not holding a prayer book. She was dressed in deepest black, in the style of full mourning that had rather gone out of fashion except, I imagined, in court circles on the most formal of occasions. Indeed, it had clearly been dug out of some old trunk or wardrobe, for its blackness was a little rusty looking. A bonnet-type hat covered her head and shaded her face, but, although I did not stare, even the swift glance I took of the woman showed me enough to recognize that she was suffering from some terrible wasting disease, for not only was she extremely pale, even more than a contrast with the blackness of her garments could account for, but the skin and, it seemed, only the thinnest layer of flesh was **tautly** stretched and strained across her bones, so that it gleamed with a curious, blue-white **sheen**, and her eyes seemed sunken back into her head. Her hands that rested on the **pew** before her were in a similar state, as though she was the victim of starvation… it seemed **poignant** that a woman who was perhaps only a short time away from her own death, should drag herself to the funeral of another…

I heard the slight rustle of clothing once more and realized that the unknown woman had already slipped quickly away, and gone out to the waiting, open grave, though to stand some yards back, beside another headstone, that was overgrown with moss and upon which she leaned slightly.

Her appearance… was so pathetically wasted, so pale and **gaunt** with disease, that it would not have been a kindness to gaze upon her; for there was still some faint trace on her features, some lingering hint, of a not inconsiderable former beauty, which must make her feel her present condition all the more keenly, as would the victim of a **smallpox**, or of some dreadful disfigurement of burning.

I saw that Mr Jerome waited for me politely in the lane, and I went quickly out after him.

'Tell me, that other woman…' I said as I reached his side, 'I hope she can find her own way home… she looked so dreadfully unwell. Who was she?'

He frowned.

'The young woman with the wasted face,' I urged, 'at the back of the church and then in the graveyard a few yards away from us.'

Mr Jerome stopped dead. He was staring at me.

📖 Glossary

discreetly carefully, so as not to draw attention to oneself

mourner person who attends a funeral

tautly tightly

sheen glow

pew long wooden seat in a church

poignant sad or upsetting

gaunt thin

smallpox a deadly disease, the rash from which often left scars on a survivor's skin

Extract 3 from *Mayhem*
by Sarah Pinborough

Suddenly I felt a chill in the pit of my stomach. Harrington flinched, and his eyes drifted, looking confused for a moment. Then his spine stiffened as *something* shifted behind him – and then he refocused.

He frowned, picking up his knife and fork and cut angrily into the remains of his beef before thrusting a large chunk into his mouth. A greasy trickle of pink liquid ran down to his chin as he chewed hungrily, but he ignored it. As his lips smacked together, it clung to the **contours** of his skin and slid down to his neck.

My eyes followed it, my attention focused on the blood so that I did not have to look at the darkness that was creeping up over Harrington's shoulder. My heart raced and I swallowed hard as a black tongue smelling of something rotten darted around Harrington's neck and squeezed like a **garrotte** for a moment before pulling back, licking up the blood as it did so.

I was assaulted by the thick, sickly stench of stagnant water, which coated the back of my nose and throat, making me want to gag. My collar felt tight, and I could not catch my breath. What was that *thing*, that awful dark shape that was too dense behind him? The **bulbous** growth was just out of sight, but my eyes hurt just trying to look at it, the sharp pains stabbing behind my eye forcing me to blink rapidly.

Harrington continued to eat, refilling his plate from the bowl of buttered potatoes in front of him and cramming them into his mouth two and three at a time. I had seen him eat like this before, and had thought there was something unnatural about it then. Now I knew why.

My ears buzzed with the noise of Juliana and Mary's chatter, but I could not make out their words. I felt distant from them, a world apart, as if I were lost under the Thames and they were still on the surface.

The *Upir* was showing itself. It clung to Harrington's shoulder, dark talons gripping him as it peered around the back of his neck, an awful **parody** of a baby carried in a sling behind its mother, that style so often seen amongst the **Orientals**.

It did not emerge fully, and only one side of its face was visible. That eye came to rest on me and I could feel my heart pounding rapidly. I tried to stay focused on Harrington; unlike the red orb that glared angrily at me from the apex of his neck and shoulder, the man's eyes were blue, and wholly human. I concentrated on them, rather than the awful wickedness in the corner of my vision, for I could not bear to look directly – even if I had had that desire, I *could not*, for it was death; it was madness; it was everything that was wrong with the world, all wrapped up into a dense black shape. The whole world's shadow had been sucked into this awful clinging **gargoyle**.

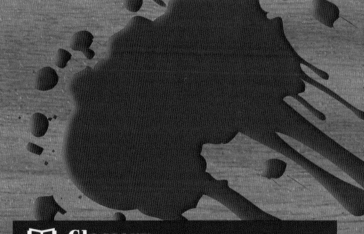

📖 Glossary

contours outline, like lines on a map that show the shape and height of the landscape

garrotte cord or wire used for strangling a victim

bulbous bulging in shape

parody imitation that is exaggerated, often for comic effect

Orientals people from Asia (term used in Victorian times, when this novel is set)

gargoyle grotesque carved face or figure attached to a gutter

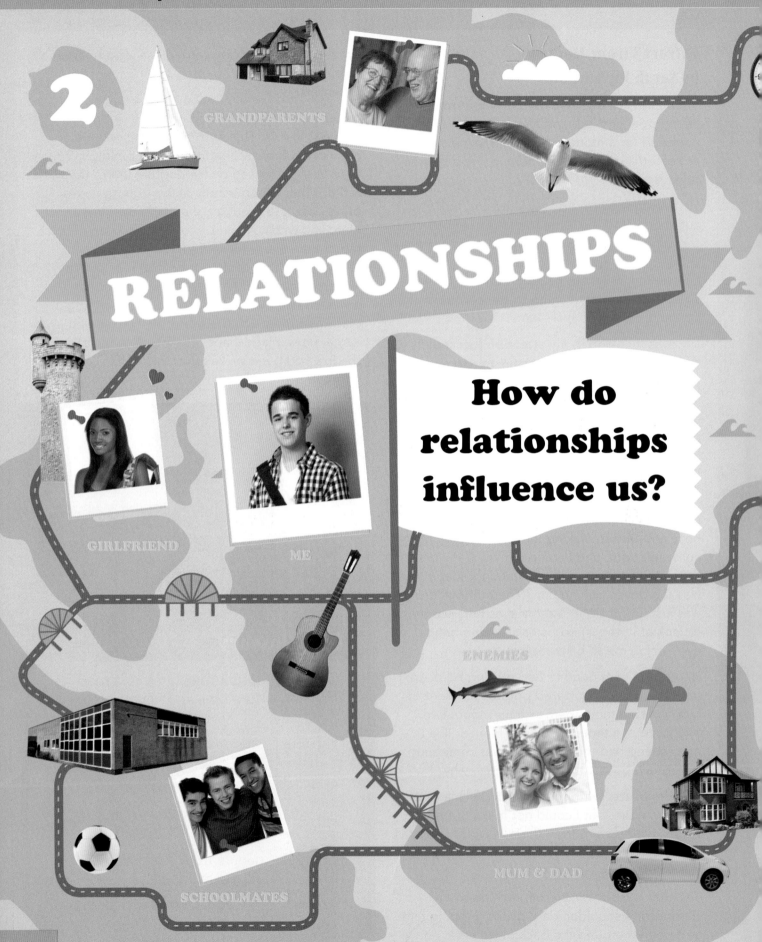

2

GRANDPARENTS

RELATIONSHIPS

How do relationships influence us?

GIRLFRIEND

ME

ENEMIES

SCHOOLMATES

MUM & DAD

Introduction

The poet John Donne once wrote 'No man is an island'. Most people have relationships with family and friends, but not all of our relationships are the same. Some may last a lifetime and survive great physical distances, while others may start and finish over a relatively short period of time. However long they last, most people feel that relationships are an important part of their lives.

Poets, playwrights and novelists have always written about relationships to celebrate, mourn or simply to reflect on them. This unit explores some of these texts and will help you to build your own skills so that you can write your own text about a relationship that is important to you.

ignite INTERVIEW
Nick Cope, Songwriter and performer

Relationships make us who we are. So, when you are deciding to write a song or a poem or anything creative, it is one of the things that just make us tick. Think about your audience. You want to move people. You want to tell them a story.

One of the things that you need to do if you are creating, whether it is poetry or song-writing, is to be a good critic of your own stuff. And you have to edit it a lot. If you step back from it, spend a bit of time looking at it and refining it, the end result is going to be better.

✎ Activities

1 The word 'relationship' means 'connection'. We have connections with all sorts of people.

Think about all the people with whom you have connections. Draw a diagram like the one on the left to show the relationships clearly.

2 Choose one of the relationships in your diagram and talk about it with a partner. For example, you could explain how you met this person and why they are important to you.

1 First Relationships

↻ Objective

Develop an interpretation of a poem, exploring the use of figurative language.

ignite INTERVIEW

ignite INTERVIEW

'Whether it is family or friends, you are who you are because of your interaction with people.'

Nick Cope

The first relationships we have are with our parents or carers. These relationships are often close, but that doesn't mean there aren't any disagreements!

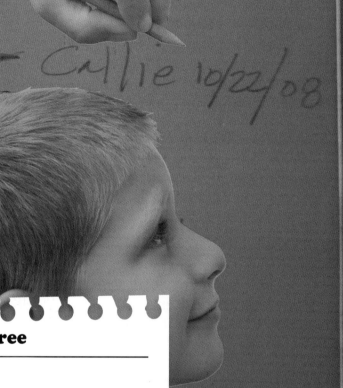

✎ Activities

1 Think about your parents or carers. Make a list of the things that you agree on and another list of things you disagree about.

Agree	Disagree
Dad's roast dinners are the best.	Bedtime
Holidays near the sea	I want a dog but Nan doesn't.

2 Read the poem on page 35. Write a brief summary about what is happening in the poem. (Think about the setting and what the mother and son are doing.)

3 The **literal** meaning of a poem is often different from the **figurative** meaning. What is the poet saying about his relationship with his mother?

📖 Glossary

literal   taking words in their usual or most basic sense

figurative   using words to convey something beyond their immediate obvious meaning; metaphorical

tweet   a short message with a maximum of 140 characters used on the social networking site Twitter

4 One of the ways in which writers present their ideas is through their choices of individual words which conjure up specific images. Look at the words 'Anchor. Kite'. Explain why you think Armitage chose those particular words. (Hint: think about what anchors and kites do.)

Extract from 'Mother Any Distance' by Simon Armitage

Mother, any distance greater than a single span

requires a second pair of hands.

You come to help me measure windows, pelmets, doors,

the acres of the walls, the prairies of the floors.

You at the zero-end, me with the spool of tape, recording

length, reporting metres, centimetres back to base, then leaving

up the stairs, the line still feeding out, unreeling

years between us. Anchor. Kite.

I space-walk through the empty bedrooms, climb

the ladder to the loft, to breaking point, where something has to give;

two floors below your fingertips still pinch

the last one-hundredth of an inch… I reach

towards a hatch that opens on an endless sky to fall or fly.

🕐 Extra Time

Poets are skilled in creating effects using carefully chosen words and phrases in a succinct, focused style. The same skills are valuable when micro blogging. Write a **tweet** of no more than 140 characters in which you explain or suggest what your parents mean to you. Use figurative language if you wish.

12 Years

start Secondary school

11 Years

10 Years

9 Years

8 Years

7 Years

6 Years

5 Years

Learned to ride a bike

4 Years

3 Years

2 Mexican Bean

Objective

Analyse the use of imagery in conveying meaning to the reader.

We were all someone's baby and many of us will become parents ourselves. In the poem 'You're', Sylvia Plath describes her child through a series of images.

Activities

1 Read the poem on page 37. What exactly is the poet describing? How old is her child?

2 Plath uses **metaphors** and **similes** to describe different aspects of her baby. Choose one simile and one metaphor and explain the comparison or description. What does it suggest to the reader?

Support

What does the metaphor 'my little loaf' suggest about the baby? What does the simile 'Snug as a bud' suggest?

3 Plath often hyphenates words in her poems in order to condense their meaning or the image into the fewest words possible. What image does the description 'moon-skulled' conjure up?

Stretch

Explain how 'Bent-backed Atlas' creates a powerful image.

4 How do you think Plath feels about her baby? Explain your answer using evidence from the poem.

'You're' by Sylvia Plath

Clownlike, happiest on your hands,

Feet to the stars, and moon-skulled,

Gilled like a fish. A common-sense

Thumbs-down on the dodo's mode.

Wrapped up in yourself like a spool,

Trawling your dark, as owls do.

Mute as a turnip from the Fourth

Of July to All Fools' Day,

O high-riser, my little loaf.

Vague as fog and looked for like mail.

Farther off than Australia.

Bent-backed Atlas, our traveled prawn.

Snug as a bud and at home

Like a sprat in a pickle jug.

A creel of eels, all ripples.

Jumpy as a Mexican bean.

Right, like a well-done sum.

A clean slate, with your own face on.

📖 Glossary

metaphor describing something as something else, not meant to be taken literally, e.g. *You are a star.*

simile a comparison that uses the words 'like' or 'as', e.g. *as white as snow*

alliteration words near each other that begin with the same sound, e.g. <u>s</u>ilken <u>s</u>leeve

assonance words near each other that have the same vowel sounds, e.g. *ben<u>ea</u>th the <u>sea</u>*

5a In pairs or small groups, prepare a reading of this poem.

- Use the punctuation to guide you.

- Decide how to divide the poem between you. You might want to recite alternate images or sentences, or take one verse each.

- Look for patterns of sound that you should emphasize, e.g. **alliteration** and **assonance**.

Prepare to answer questions on your reading. Consider the following question:

How does the imagery come alive through reading the poem?

5b Read the poem aloud to another group or to the class. Take feedback and answer any questions on your reading of the poem.

3 Best Friends

↻ Objective

Explore ideas and reflect on feelings through discussion with others.

'Three' by Chrissie Gittins

My best friend has a best friend,

She is a bester friend than me,

But when they have a falling out

My friend is best with me.

📖 Activities

1 Read the poem above. What can you remember about your first best friend? Note down your memories.

2a Read the newspaper article on page 39. Look at any unfamiliar words in the text. Try to work out their meaning from the context and by thinking about similar words. Check your answers in a dictionary.

2b Write a new title for this article that is shorter and snappier, and sums up the **theme** of the article.

📚 Support

You might want to consider making use of alliteration in your title.

3a Prepare for a debate about whether best friends should be banned.

- Decide whether you agree or disagree with the Head Teacher.
- List your arguments to back up your viewpoint.
- Think of examples to illustrate what you say.
- Rehearse what you want to say, remembering to speak clearly and slowly, using pauses for effect and emphasizing key words.

↔ Stretch

Try to anticipate some of the arguments on the other side and decide how you would counter those arguments.

3b Present your views in a debate.

CHILDREN SHOULDN'T HAVE BEST FRIENDS
PRIVATE SCHOOL HEAD ARGUES

Young children should not have best friends because it could leave others feeling ostracised and hurt, the headmaster of a leading prep school has said. Instead they should be encouraged to have 'lots of good friends' to avoid overly possessive relationships and upsetting fall-outs.

Some parents of pupils at Thomas's private day school in Battersea, South-West London, have been told that their children cannot have best friends, *The Telegraph* understands. Ben Thomas, the school's headmaster, said there was no official policy to that effect but he supported the idea.

He said: 'There is sound judgement behind it. You can get very possessive friendships, and it is much easier if they share friendships and have a wide range of good friends rather than obsessing too much about who their best friend is.'...

Parents and nannies collecting pupils from the school on Wednesday were divided on the idea of discouraging children from having best friends, with some describing it as 'ridiculous' while others welcomed it.

'You have to have best friends, it is all part of learning the ways of life,' said one, who declined to be named. 'I left school years ago but some of my best friends today are ones I made when I was quite young. That is just silly, not having best friends.'

But another parent, who did not want to give her name, said: 'I think it is sensible, particularly in London where there is so much movement. We have all seen the disappointment when a "best friend" leaves. It is much better if they have a good range of friends.'

☑ **Progress Check**

Reflect on whether you:

- listened carefully to what others said
- responded to their ideas and viewpoints
- presented your own ideas clearly and logically.

📖 **Glossary**

theme subject or main idea

4 Making Time

↻ Objective

Explore how setting and dialogue can help to convey an author's message.

Although our first relationships are with our parents or carers, some of our closest relationships are with our friends. These are often the people with whom we share our deepest secrets and favourite moments in life.

10

✎ Activities

1 Over the centuries, people have had various views about the importance of friendship. Read and discuss the three quotations on the right. To what extent do you agree or disagree with them? Give examples from your own experience to support your ideas.

17

ignite INTERVIEW

'When you are creating things the end result might not quite work. But it shouldn't put you off, because each time you learn something.'

Nick Cope

1
Friendship is a single soul dwelling in two bodies.
Aristotle

2
It is one of the blessings of old friends that you can afford to be stupid with them.
Ralph Waldo Emerson

3
Friendship is unnecessary, like philosophy, like art... It has no survival value; rather it is one of those things that give value to survival.
C. S. Lewis

22

It is easy to take our friends for granted. We all have to remember to make time for them, however busy we are.

2a Read the poem on the right. What is the poet saying about his relationship with his friend? Explain your answer, giving details from the poem.

2b Do you think that the poet's attitude to his friend is right? Explain why, giving examples from your own experience.

3 In pairs, plan and prepare two contrasting short role-plays. Both should be in the same setting with the same two people, but each one should show a different attitude between two people. Think carefully about:

- where the action is set
- what each person is doing
- how they react to each other and what they say
- what this illustrates about friendship.

'A Time to Talk' by Robert Frost

When a friend calls to me from the road

And slows his horse to a meaning walk,

I don't stand still and look around

On all the hills I haven't hoed,

And shout from where I am, 'What is it?'

No, not as there is a time to talk.

I thrust my hoe in the mellow ground,

Blade-end up and five feet tall,

And plod: I go up to the stone wall

For a friendly visit.

☑ **Progress Check**

Act out your scenes. Ask your audience to rate you on a scale of 1–3 (3 being the highest score) on how well you:

- used dialogue and action to reveal the relationship
- conveyed a clear message about friendship in the two contrasting scenes.

Invite them to suggest one area that could be improved.

5 The Wrong Clothes

↻ Objective

Understand how spoken language can reflect a character's background and social status.

Friendship has always been a popular theme in stories. From *The Epic of Gilgamesh*, the oldest recorded story in the world, to Harry Potter, friendship has played a central part in story-telling.

📖 Activities

1 Make a list of as many friendships in literature (stories and plays) as you can.

2 Discuss why you think friendship is such a popular theme.

The extract on page 43 is from *Great Expectations* by Charles Dickens. The story follows the life of Pip, brought up by his stern sister and gentle, blacksmith brother-in-law, Joe Gargery. As Pip's fortunes change, he moves to London, becomes better educated and finds new, rich, smart friends. When Joe comes to visit, Pip is ashamed and embarrassed by Joe's awkward, country manners. Joe senses Pip's snobbery, but that doesn't lessen his affection for him, as he makes clear in his parting speech.

Extract from *Great Expectations* by Charles Dickens

'Pip, dear old chap, life is made of ever so many partings welded together, as I may say, and one man's a blacksmith, and one's a whitesmith, and one's a goldsmith, and one's a coppersmith. Diwisions among such must come, and must be met as they come. If there's been any fault at all to-day, it's mine. You and me is not two figures to be together in London; nor yet anywheres else but what is private, and beknown, and understood among friends. It ain't that I am proud, but that I want to be right, as you shall never see me no more in these clothes. I'm wrong in these clothes. I'm wrong out of the forge, the kitchen, or off th' meshes. You won't find half so much fault in me if you think of me in my forge dress, with my hammer in my hand, or even my pipe. You won't find half so much fault in me if, supposing as you should ever wish to see me, you come and put your head in at the forge window and see Joe the blacksmith, there, at the old anvil, in the old burnt apron, sticking to the old work. I'm awful dull, but I hope I've beat out something nigh the rights of this at last. And so GOD bless you, dear old Pip, old chap, GOD bless you!'

I had not been mistaken in my fancy that there was a simple dignity in him. The fashion of his dress could no more come in its way when he spoke these words, than it could come in its way in Heaven. He touched me gently on the forehead, and went out. As soon as I could recover myself sufficiently, I hurried out after him and looked for him in the neighbouring streets; but he was gone.

3 How can you tell that Joe's speech includes non-standard English? Think about vocabulary, informality and **dialect**. What does it reveal about Joe?

4 Now think about what Joe is actually saying (rather than his style of talking). In your own words, explain what he means.

5 What do we learn about Pip in this extract? How does he react to Joe's speech? What do you think he is feeling?

6 Draw up a list of reasons why friendships change over time. Take one of these reasons and use it as the basis for a short story, poem or teen webpage article. Plan your writing before starting to write.

📖 Glossary

dialect informal words used in a specific geographical area

🕐 Extra Time

SPAG

Read through your Activity 6 writing piece. What improvements can you make? Check your spelling, punctuation and grammar.

6 Loss

Objective

Draw on knowledge, literary techniques, style and structure to draft a poem.

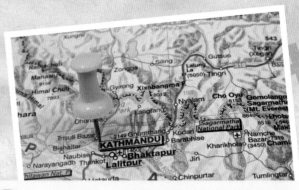

The loss of a friend or relative can be painful. Read the poem on page 45. Decide whether it mourns or celebrates Meg.

✎ Activities

1a Who is the narrator of the poem and to whom is she speaking?

1b How would you describe the **tone** of the poem? Explain your answer with examples from the poem.

❖ Support

Decide whether the poem is formal or informal; serious or light-hearted; happy or sad.

1c Why do you think the poet wrote the final lines as a separate couplet? What does 'all the king's horses' refer to?

1d What do we learn about Meg in this poem?

📖 Glossary

tone atmosphere

2 Adcock remembers some good times she had with her friend and uses these to structure her poem and to celebrate what she admired in her friend. Plan your own short poem about a friend or relative, using a similar style,

- Choose an experience that you shared.

- Address your poem to that friend or relative.

- Use an informal style.

- Celebrate something about your friend or relative in recounting the experience, e.g. their sense of humour, kindness, bravery, fun, mischief, loyalty.

- Include a final couplet to sum up your thoughts.

☑ Progress Check

Swap your first draft with a partner. Ask them to comment on two aspects of your poem that they think are strong and to suggest one area for improvement. Aspects they might consider are:

- description of an event

- depiction of your friend or relative

- consistent tone throughout

- use of vocabulary.

'For Meg' by Fleur Adcock

Half the things you did were too scary for me.
Skiing? No thanks. Riding? I've never learnt.
Canoeing? I'd be sure to tip myself out
and stagger home, ignominiously wet.
It was my son, that time in Kathmandu,
who galloped off with you to the temple at Bodnath
in a monsoon downpour, both of you on horses
from the King of Nepal's stables. Not me.

And as for the elephants – my God, the elephants!
How did you get me up on to one of those?
First they lay down; the way to climb aboard
was to walk up a gross leg, then straddle a sack
(that's all there was to sit on), while the creature
wobbled and swayed through the jungle for slow hours.
It felt like riding on the dome of St Paul's
in an earthquake. This was supposed to be a treat.

You and Alex and Maya, in her best sari,
sat beaming at the wildlife, you with your camera
proficiently clicking. You were pregnant at the time.
I clung with both hot hands to the bit of rope
that was all there was to cling to. The jungle steamed.
As soon as we were back in sight of the camp
I got off and walked through a river to reach it.
You laughed, but kindly. We couldn't all be like you.

Now you've done the scariest thing there is;
and all the king's horses, dear Meg, won't bring you back.

7 Without You

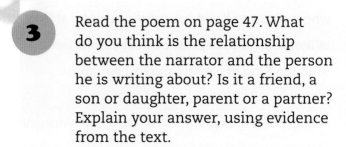

↻ Objective

Explore how repetition and diversity of imagery can build up poetic structure.

✎ Activities

1 Discuss how it feels when someone you care about goes away. Decide on three adjectives to sum up those feelings. (You can't use 'sad', 'unhappy' or 'lonely'!)

Adrian Henri was an artist as well as a poet. He called himself a 'notebook poet', writing down ideas all the time and then turning them into poems. Read his poems below and on page 47, thinking about how his description as a 'notebook poet' helps to explain the structure and form of his poems.

Extract from 'Love is...' by Adrian Henri

Love is you and love is me

Love is a prison and love is free

Love's what's there when you're away from me

Love is.

2 Using the extract from 'Love is...' as a starting point, write the next two stanzas. Use rhyme if you wish to, but the last line of each stanza should be just 'Love is.'

3 Read the poem on page 47. What do you think is the relationship between the narrator and the person he is writing about? Is it a friend, a son or daughter, parent or a partner? Explain your answer, using evidence from the text.

4 Look at the lines about 'stillborn poems', 'indifferent colonels' and 'Mahler's 8th'. Using the context, explain what you think these phrases mean.

5 Choose one or two images that you feel conjure up particularly powerful visual pictures. Explain how they make an impact on the reader, e.g. are they particularly violent, unlikely or humorous?

'Without You' by Adrian Henri

Without you every morning would feel like going back to work after a holiday,

Without you I couldn't stand the smell of the East Lancs Road,

Without you ghost ferries would cross the Mersey manned by skeleton crews,

Without you I'd probably feel happy and have more money and time and nothing to do with it,

Without you I'd have to leave my stillborn poems on other people's doorsteps, wrapped in brown paper,

Without you there'd never be sauce to put on sausage butties,

Without you plastic flowers in shop windows would just be plastic flowers in shop windows

Without you I'd spend my summers picking morosely over the remains of train crashes,

Without you white birds would wrench themselves free from my paintings and fly off dripping blood into the night,

Without you green apples wouldn't taste greener,

Without you Mothers wouldn't let their children play out after tea,

Without you every musician in the world would forget how to play the blues,

Without you Public Houses would be public again,

Without you the Sunday Times colour supplement would come out in black-and-white,

Without you indifferent colonels would shrug their shoulders and press the button,

Without you they'd stop changing the flowers in Piccadilly Gardens,

Without you Clark Kent would forget how to become Superman,

Without you Sunshine Breakfast would only consist of Cornflakes,

Without you there'd be no colour in Magic colouring books

Without you Mahler's 8th would only be performed by street musicians in derelict houses,

Without you they'd forget to put the salt in every packet of crisps,

Without you it would be an offence punishable by a fine of up to £200 or two months' imprisonment to be found in possession of curry powder,

Without you riot police are massing in quiet sidestreets,

Without you all streets would be one-way the other way,

Without you there'd be no one not to kiss goodnight when we quarrel,

Without you the first martian to land would turn round and go away again,

Without you they'd forget to change the weather,

Without you blind men would sell unlucky heather,

Without you there would be

no landscapes/no stations/no houses,

no chipshops/no quiet villages/no seagulls

on beaches/no hopscotch on pavements/no night/no morning/

there'd be no city no country

Without you.

8 Not a Fairy Tale Romance...

↻ Objective

Understand how traditional forms can be adapted to convey a contemporary message.

◣ Activities

1 Write down what you think are the key ingredients of a traditional fairy tale.

2 Look at the title of the poem on page 49. It is a combination of two fairy tales. What are they? Share your knowledge of these stories with a partner.

Fairy tales encourage us to believe that romantic relationships can last a lifetime, although the reality is often very different. Read 'Rapunzstiltskin' on page 49, thinking about how it compares with traditional retellings of these stories.

3 How do the maiden and the prince differ from their traditional personalities?

4a The poet refers to the prince's 'tendency to talk in strung-together cliché'. Make a list of all the **clichés** in the poem.

4b Why do you think the poet has used all of these clichés in one poem? What is she saying about romantic relationships?

↔ Stretch

What do you think the poet is saying about love poems and fairy tales?

📖 Glossary

cliché an expression which is so overused that it has little meaning

'Rapunzstiltskin' by Liz Lochhead

& just when our maiden had got

good & used to her isolation,

stopped daily expecting to be rescued,

had come to *almost* love her tower,

along comes This Prince

with absolutely

all the wrong answers.

Of course she had not been brought up to look for

originality or gingerbread

so at first she was quite undaunted

by his tendency to talk in strung-together cliché.

'Just hang on and we'll get you out of there'

he hollered like a fireman in some soap opera

when she confided her plight (the old

hag inside etc. & how trapped she was);

well, it was corny but

he did look sort of gorgeous

axe and all.

So there she was, humming & pulling,

all the pins out of her chignon,

throwing him all the usual lifelines

til, soon, he was shimmying in & out

every other day as though

he owned the place, bringing her

the women's mags & skeins of silk

from which she was meant, eventually,

to weave the means of her own escape.

'All very well & good' she prompted,

'but when exactly?'

She gave him til

well past the bell on the timeclock.

She mouthed at him, hinted,

she was keener than a TV quizmaster

that he should get it right

'I'll do everything in my power' he intoned, *'but*

the impossible (she groaned) *might*

take a little longer.' He grinned.

She pulled her glasses off.

'All the better

to see you with my dear?' he hazarded.

She screamed, cut off her hair.

'Why, you're beautiful?' He guessed tentatively.

'No, No, No!' she

shrieked & stamped her foot so

hard it sank six cubits through the floorboards.

'I love you?' he came up with

as finally she tore herself in two.

🕐 Extra Time

Imagine you are either the maiden or the prince, writing updates on your social networking page as your feelings develop during the poem. Include some of your posts and comments from friends who may be reading them.

9 Is Love Blind?

Objective

Compare texts written in the same literary tradition.

Activities

1a Look at the image on the right. Make a list of adjectives to describe each person.

1b When we are in love, we tend to see only the best in our partner. Add some more words to your lists which make these people seem more perfect than they actually are.

Read the love **sonnet** on page 51. It was written in 1596. Use the annotations to help explain the references that would have been familiar to educated readers of the time.

2 What does the poet want us to understand about his feelings for this woman?

3 How accurate would you judge his descriptions to be? Use evidence from the text to explain your view.

📖 Glossary

sonnet a 14-line poetic form with a strict rhyme scheme and structure which originated in Italy in the 13th century, and means 'little song'. It became a popular form for love poetry in the 16th century.

'Fidessa' by Bartholemew Griffin

My Lady's hair is threads of beaten gold;

Her front, the purest, crystal eye hath seen;

Her eyes, the brightest stars the heavens hold;

Her cheeks, red roses, such as seld have been; → Few

Her pretty lips, of red vermilion dye;

Her hand, of ivory the purest white;

Her blush, AURORA, or the morning sky. → Goddess of the dawn

Her breast displays two silver fountains bright;

The spheres, her voice; her grace, the Graces three; ← Representations of beauty, charm and joy

Her body is the saint that I adore;

Her smiles and favours, sweet as honey be.

Her feet, fair THETIS praiseth evermore. ← Goddess of water

But ah, the worst and last is yet behind:

For of a griffon she doth bear the mind! ← A creature known for its power and majesty, suggesting the woman is out of his reach

During medieval times, a tradition of **courtly love** developed as a way of expressing love in a noble and **chivalrous** way. Marriage in this period was seen as a means of gaining power and wealth, rather than being about love, so it was common for people to have romantic relationships outside marriage.

The rules of courtly love were listed by Andreas Capellanus in the 12th century. Read the extract on the right.

4 Discuss what you have learned about courtly love. How do you think the tradition of courtly love is reflected in the sonnet 'Fidessa'? Give examples.

The rules of courtly love:

- A lover is obsessed with how his love looks.
- It is wrong to love a woman who you would be ashamed to marry.
- If you win your beloved too easily, that makes them less valuable. If they appear unobtainable, they are more valuable.
- When you are in love, you can't eat or sleep properly.
- Someone in love can think of nothing but their beloved.

📖 Glossary

courtly love   a type of love between members of the nobility, carried out in secret

chivalrous   considerate and courteous

More to explore

William Shakespeare wrote over 150 sonnets. Many followed the traditional style of love sonnets, but there were exceptions. Read 'Sonnet 130', which is a **parody** of the courtly love sonnet.

'Sonnet 130'
by William Shakespeare

My mistress' eyes are nothing like the sun;
Coral is far more red, than her lips' red:
If snow be white, why then her breasts are **dun**;
If hairs be wires, black wires grow on her head.
I have seen roses **damasked**, red and white,
But no such roses see I in her cheeks;
And in some perfumes is there more delight
Than in the breath that from my mistress reeks.
I love to hear her speak, yet well I know
That music hath a far more pleasing sound:
I grant I never saw a goddess go,
My mistress, when she walks, treads on the ground:
And yet by heaven, I think my love as rare,
As any she belied with false compare.

Activities continued

5 With close reference to the sonnet, explain what you think Shakespeare is trying to achieve.

Glossary

parody imitation that is exaggerated, often for comic effect

dun beige

damasked patterned

6 Write a short comparison of the two sonnets on pages 51 and 52. Think about:

- how the poets feel about their mistresses

- how they use different methods to present their relationships.

You may find it helpful to complete a grid, like the one started below, to help you organize your ideas for your comparison.

'Fidessa'			'Sonnet 130'		
Physical and emotional qualities		Traditional courtly love?	Physical and emotional qualities		Traditional courtly love?
Evidence	Effect		Evidence	Effect	
Hair is threads of beaten gold.	Description suggests high value and extreme craftsmanship	Yes	Black wires grow on her head.	Unflattering, almost comical image	No

Support

Plan your writing in paragraphs. Remember to include an introduction and conclusion, as well as your main comparison paragraphs. You might want to use phrases such as:

- On the other hand…

- Whereas both poets…

- In contrast…

- To sum up, although both poets…

Glossary

syllable a word or part of a word that has one vowel sound when you say it, e.g. 'cat' has one syllable, 'din-o-saur' has three syllables

Stretch

What do the sonnets have in common in terms of structure and form? Look at the rhyme scheme and number of **syllables** in each line.

10 Assessment: Writing a Poem About Family or Friends

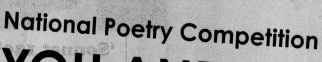

National Poetry Competition
YOU AND I...

A national media company is launching a poetry competition for young people aged between 12 and 16. The competition is called 'You and I...' and the company is inviting young people to submit poems based on a relationship between two people – they can be friends, family, girlfriends, boyfriends or even enemies!

The poems will be judged partly by a panel made up of publishers, poets and media producers, and partly by a public voting system. The winning entries will be broadcast on national TV and radio, and the poets will be invited to read their poems at a prestigious literary festival.

The judges will be looking for skills in:

- expressing something entertaining, unusual or touching about a relationship
- using imagery to conjure up pictures in the reader's mind
- employing poetic devices to create interesting effects
- choosing a structure and form suitable to convey the message of the poem (as well as traditional poem forms, you could consider free verse, rap or performance poetry)
- using interesting, varied vocabulary.

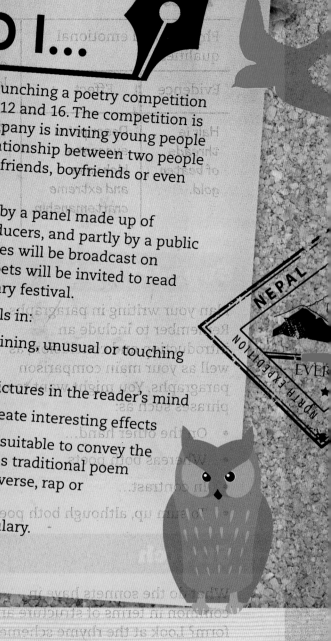

Before you write...

Plan: Think about what you have learned in this unit, both about poetic conventions and the portrayal of different types of relationships. Consider various relationships that you could focus on, jotting down what sort of approach you could take, before deciding on which one to choose. Think about the tone and mood of the poem you want to write and note down any particular vocabulary or phrases which come to mind.

As you write...

Review and edit: Keep reading and re-reading your work, both to yourself and aloud. Think about the sound of your poem as well as its meaning. Leave gaps where you are stuck for words and come back to them later. Experiment with alternative words and expressions in order to find the most original and apt language. Keep your audience in mind, checking that you are creating the effects you want.

When you have finished writing...

Proofread: Check that what you have written is clear and accurate with correct spelling and punctuation that helps the reader to know how to read the poem aloud. Check particularly for errors that you know you tend to make in your writing.

ignite INTERVIEW

'If you take a bit of time to step back from what you have created and have a really good look at it, refining it, the end result is going to be better.'

Nick Cope

3
Exploring Difference

How does it feel to stand out from the crowd?

Introduction

We aren't all the same, but do we want to be? How does it feel to stand out from the crowd? Over the centuries many writers and artists have used their talents to explore and celebrate difference.

In this unit, you will read powerful and challenging pieces of fiction, non-fiction and poetry which explore what it is like to be different. You will analyse how writing can challenge perceptions, help us to empathize with others, and celebrate the lives of those who stand out from the crowd.

ignite INTERVIEW
Nikki Emerson, Wheelchair track athlete

I broke my back in a car accident in 2008 and the Beijing Paralympics inspired me to get into sport and to try and reach the highest level that I could. When I was at school, I wanted to fit in. After I broke my back and I realized I couldn't be the same as everyone else, I started to think more about what being different meant. But being in a wheelchair I don't think is what makes me different. I train really hard as an athlete, I have been successful in my corporate career and the feeling of representing Great Britain for the first time will stay with me for ever.

✎ Activities

1 How does our society treat people who are seen to be different? Do you think we are a tolerant or intolerant society?

2 Discuss any books, films or TV programmes you have read or watched that deal with difference. What did they help you understand about the experience of being different?

1 Challenging Perceptions

↻ Objectives

- Consider and discuss how works of art can challenge perceptions.

- Give a presentation expressing a viewpoint.

Works of art, such as paintings and sculptures, can sometimes help you to see a subject in a new light. Read the newspaper article on page 59 about the exhibition of the statue Alison Lapper Pregnant on a plinth in London's Trafalgar Square, and then complete the activities below.

ignite INTERVIEW

'As someone who is disabled, I would say that my biggest problem with the way that society treats people that are different is how much they highlight it.'

Nikki Emerson

✎ Activities

1 Using the article opposite and your own views, discuss the following questions.

- Was Alison Lapper right to pose for the sculpture?

- Should it have been exhibited in such a prominent place?

- Do you think that it might have changed some people's attitudes to disability?

During the discussion, make sure you explore what other people say to consider different points of view.

2 Imagine that you are the artist, Marc Quinn, and that you have been asked to appear before a committee who will decide which sculptures will be exhibited on the plinth. Create a presentation to persuade the committee to choose your statue.

📖 Glossary

congenital disorder   a medical condition existing at birth or that develops during the first month of life

defiance   resisting what is expected of you

CONTROVERSIAL STATUE
UNVEILED IN TRAFALGAR SQUARE

The controversial statue of disabled artist Alison Lapper has been officially unveiled on Trafalgar Square's fourth plinth.

Marc Quinn's 13-tonne, 11ft 6in high, white marble sculpture is London's latest landmark.

Lapper, who was born with no arms and shortened legs due to a **congenital disorder**, posed naked for Quinn when she was eight months pregnant.

London Mayor Ken Livingstone hailed Lapper as a 'modern heroine'.

He said the statue, titled Alison Lapper Pregnant, made a worthy companion to Nelson's Column.

'This square celebrates the courage of men in battle. Alison's life is a struggle to overcome much greater difficulties than many of the men we celebrate and commemorate here,' he said.

'Marc Quinn has created an artwork that is a potent symbol and a great addition to London.

'It is a work about courage, beauty and **defiance**, which both captures and represents all that is best about our great city.

'Alison Lapper Pregnant is a modern heroine – strong, formidable and full of hope. It is a great artwork for London and for the world.'

The artist and his subject attended the unveiling ceremony in a rainy Trafalgar Square.

'An amazing day'

Lapper, there with her five-year-old son Parys, said: 'This is an amazing day for me, not only just for me but for all the people in the country

and across the world who have got a disability. It's a really positive sculpture and an important step forward.

'We have been hidden away for way too long. It's about time people started to confront their prejudice.

'It's a real honour to be up there.'

Quinn said: 'I regard it as a modern tribute to femininity, disability and motherhood. It is so rare to see disability in everyday life – let alone naked, pregnant and proud.

'The sculpture makes the ultimate statement about disability – that it can be as beautiful and valid a form of being as any other.'

2 A Different Child

↺ Objective

Identify the techniques used by a writer to convey thoughts and emotions.

Writing can allow people to express their emotions with great power and clarity. The letter that begins on page 62 is written by the mother of an autistic child. It appeared in the 'Family' section of *The Guardian* newspaper, as part of a series in which readers are encouraged to write an imaginary letter to someone important in their life.

✎ Activities
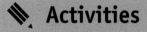

1 As you read the letter, think about:

- why the mother might have wanted to write it

- who the audience for this letter is

- how the author might want her writing to affect her readers.

📖 Glossary

figurative language   words and phrases used to enhance meaning, e.g. using simile or metaphor to make comparisons, using imagery to heighten the impact of what is written, etc.

2 How does the writer use **figurative language** to express her emotions towards her son? Pick out examples and explain how they help you to understand the mother's feelings.

▣ Support

For example, in the opening paragraph the writer talks about her son being 'wrenched' from the 'warmth' of the womb into the 'cold' world. These three words are used figuratively to indicate the violence of the birth and the shock experienced by the baby, suggesting her concern for him.

3a Re-read the letter. Think of a different word to describe the emotion of each paragraph.

🗇 Support

Did you use the word 'love' more than once? If so, did it mean precisely the same thing each time?

3b The paragraphs provide the structure for the letter. What does the structure show about the writer's relationship with her son?

↔ Stretch

Explain what the mother means when she says 'I mourned for the loss... of an imagined future.'

4 Write your own letter to someone important in your life. Use figurative language to express your feelings about that person.

DAILY NEWS

World · Business · Finan... · Lifestyle · Travel · S...

...LLING NATIONAL NEWSPAP...

THE...

Issue: 240104

First Edition

MUM

More to explore

A letter to...
my beautiful blue-eyed boy

You were born on Christmas Day 2002, wrenched from the warmth of my womb, into this harsh, cold, **judgmental** world. You were placed on my empty belly covered in blood, your little chest heaved as your cry pierced the air. Your miniature body looked so perfect, your tiny hands and fingers looked like they belonged to a porcelain doll. I couldn't hold you, my beautiful baby boy, until the following morning; I am sorry that I missed the first few hours of your life.

For the next few weeks I washed, fed and cared for you, my miracle, meeting your every need and want. I knew deep within my soul that I loved you but felt that this love was just out of reach and I couldn't quite grasp its emotion. Then suddenly, one ordinary day it hit me; an explosion of emotion so strong and fast that it caught my breath and a rush of all-consuming love for you **engulfed** me.

You were a beautiful boy, happy and contented. Your sunny personality lit up my life, and of those who surrounded you. You chatted intently with everyone, greeting strangers like long lost friends, making people laugh with your **quirky** little ways and funny sayings. You ran everywhere, scampering about like a puppy, climbing everything you encountered, pushing every button you could reach, closing every door you found open. You were a clever little boy with a large vocabulary for one so young. I was so proud of you, my gorgeous boy.

As you grew, your father and I began to notice differences between other children and you – you couldn't wind down when tired, couldn't calm down when angry. You began to get obsessed by little things. Over time you began to become less contented, fretful, anxious, distant and untouchable; reacting violently when we tried to give you comforting cuddles when in distress. You would hate your own behaviour and punish yourself with words, scratches and slaps. I would try to reach into your world to ease your pain, but you wouldn't let me in. To helplessly watch you, my beautiful boy, in such torment was torture. Deep in my soul I knew that you were **inherently** different; a lost little boy living in his own world.

People no longer laughed at your quirky ways or funny sayings; my sweet boy, so wrapped up within yourself, never noticed their cruel, harsh words, their looks and their tuts that judged your every word and movement. Those hurtful, unforgivable comments wounded my heart but I was grateful for your unawareness and amazed how you chatted unaffectedly with these cold-hearted beings. You are a better person than me.

"I knew that you were inherently different"

Referred to the Child and Adolescent Mental Health Service, we filled in countless questionnaires, attended many interviews and positive parenting groups. Eventually, after this long, arduous process you had a diagnosis – **Autistic spectrum disorder**. Selfishly, for a short time, your father and I felt relieved; it wasn't us who had failed you after all. But now, my beautiful boy, you have a label, permanently pinned to your personality, which follows you like a shadow you cannot shake off.

I felt **bereaved**. I mourned for the loss of my perfect child, the loss of my hopes and aspirations, the loss of an imagined future. Then, just like the sun rises and a new day begins I realised I was mourning for a son I had never had. I look with fresh eyes at you and start to appreciate with new-found vigour everything you are and everything you can be. I feel relaxed and am conscious that I have lived these last few years as though I have been holding my breath and now, at last, I can exhale and breathe in the fresh new air.

> "I was mourning for a son I had never had"

I watch you in your own little world and I still want to wrap my arms around you, protecting you. I know that soon a mother's love will not be enough and I cannot keep you close for ever. I have to let you go. I encourage your independence, your adaptation to the real world, always outwardly smiling, never revealing the tears of raw love that rip through my heart. I am so very, very proud of you, my beautiful blue-eyed boy.

With unconditional, everlasting love,

Mum x

📖 Glossary

judgmental   ready to judge another's behaviour

engulfed   overwhelmed

quirky   odd

inherently   permanently

Autistic spectrum disorder   a condition characterized by difficulty with social and communication skills and obsessive or repetitive behaviour

bereaved   suffering the loss of a loved one

3 Free at Last

↺ Objectives

- Analyse structure by exploring the techniques used to build a sense of tension.

- Explore characterization and experiment with this in your own writing.

Christy Brown was born with cerebral palsy, unable to control any part of his body except his left foot. His inability to speak effectively cut him off from his family. In this extract from his autobiography, *My Left Foot*, Christy describes how he first tried to communicate. Read the extract on pages 66–67 and then complete the activities.

📖 Glossary

narrator's voice   the voice telling the story. In an autobiography this is usually the writer's own voice.

subordinate clause   a clause in a sentence that provides additional information but which cannot stand on its own

monologue   speech by a single character expressing their thoughts or feelings

✎ Activities

1   What impression do you get of Christy from this extract? Discuss:

- his actions and the way these are described

- his family's reactions to what he does

- the way the **narrator's voice** helps us to share his thoughts and feelings.

↔ Stretch

Re-read the paragraph beginning 'I did. I stiffened my body and put my left foot out again…'. How does the author make you feel about Christy's achievement as you read this paragraph?

2 How does the writer build up a sense of tension? Comment on the way the sentences are constructed.

SPAG

 Support

Look at the paragraph beginning 'I held it tightly between my toes...'. What do you notice about the sentence constructions used here and what effects do these create? Think about:

- the length of the sentences

- the use of **subordinate clauses**.

3 Write and perform a short **monologue** describing the events from the point of view of Christy's mother or father.

More to explore

Extract from *My Left Foot*
by Christy Brown

In a corner Mona and Paddy were sitting huddled together, a few torn **school primers** before them. They were writing down little sums on to an old chipped slate, using a bright piece of yellow chalk. I was close to them, propped up by a few pillows against the wall, watching.

It was the chalk that attracted me so much. It was a long, slender stick of vivid yellow. I had never seen anything like it before, and it showed up so well against the black surface of the slate that I was fascinated by it as much as if it had been a stick of gold.

Suddenly I wanted desperately to do what my sister was doing. Then – without thinking or knowing exactly what I was doing, I reached out and took the stick of chalk out of my sister's hand – *with my left foot.*

I do not know why I used my left foot to do this. It is a puzzle to many people as well as to myself, for, although I had displayed a curious interest in my toes at an early age, I had never attempted before this to use either of my feet in any way. That day, however, my left foot, apparently of its own **volition**, reached out and very impolitely took the chalk out of my sister's hand.

I held it tightly between my toes, and, acting on an impulse, made a wild sort of scribble with it on the slate. Next moment I stopped, a bit dazed, surprised, looking down at the stick of yellow chalk stuck between my toes, not knowing what to do with it next, hardly knowing how it got there. Then I looked up and became aware that everyone had stopped talking and were staring at me silently. Nobody stirred. Mona, her black curls framing her chubby little face, stared at me with great big eyes and open mouth. Across the open hearth, his face lit by flames, sat my father, leaning forward, hands outspread on his knees, his shoulders tense. I felt the sweat break out on my forehead.

My mother came in from the pantry with a steaming pot in her hand. She stopped midway between the table and the fire, feeling the tension flowing through the room. She followed their stare and saw me, in the corner. Her eyes looked from my face down to my foot, with the chalk gripped between my toes. She put down the pot.

Then she crossed over to me and knelt down beside me, as she had done so many times before.

'I'll show you what to do with it, Chris,' she said, very slowly and in a queer, jerky way, her face flushed as if with some inner excitement.

Taking another piece of chalk from Mona, she hesitated, then very deliberately drew on the floor in front of me, *the single letter 'A'.*

'Copy that,' she said, looking steadily at me. 'Copy it, Christy.'

I couldn't.

I looked about me, looked around at the faces that were turned towards me at that moment frozen, immobile, eager, waiting for a miracle in their midst.

The stillness was **profound**. The room was full of flame and shadow that danced before my eyes and lulled my **taut** nerves into a sort of waking sleep. I could hear the sound of the water-tap dripping in the pantry, the loud ticking of the clock on the **mantelshelf**, and the soft hiss and crackle of the logs on the open hearth.

I tried again. I put out my foot and made a wild jerking stab with the chalk which produced a very crooked line and nothing more. Mother held the slate steady for me.

'Try again, Chris,' she whispered in my ear. 'Again.'

I did. I stiffened my body and put my left foot out again, for the third time. I drew one side of the letter. I drew half the other side. Then the stick of chalk broke and I was left with a stump. I wanted to fling it away and give up. Then I felt my mother's hand on my shoulder. I tried once more. Out went my foot. I shook, I sweated and strained every muscle. My hands were so tightly clenched that my fingernails bit into the flesh. I set my teeth so hard that I nearly pierced my lower lip. Everything in the room swam till the faces around me were mere patches of white. But – I drew it – *the letter 'A'.* There it was on the floor before me. Shaky, with awkward, wobbly sides and a very uneven centre line but it was the letter 'A'. I looked up. I saw my mother's face for a moment, tears on her cheeks. Then my father stooped down and hoisted me on to his shoulder.

I had done it! I had started – the thing that was to give my mind its chance of expressing itself. True, I couldn't speak with my lips, but now I would speak through something more lasting than spoken words – written words.

That one letter, scrawled on the floor with a broken bit of yellow chalk gripped between my toes, was my road to a new world, my key to mental freedom. It was to provide a source of relaxation to the tense, taut thing that was me which panted for expression behind a twisted mouth.

📖 Glossary

school primers   school books

volition   choice

profound   deep

taut   stretched to breaking point

mantelshelf   the shelf above a fireplace

🕐 Extra Time

Read *My Left Foot* or other autobiographies by people who have overcome great challenges in their lives.

COLOURED CHALK

INCLUDES 7 PIECES OF CHALK

4 Pushing the Limits

↻ Objective

Evaluate an author's purpose and experiment with extended metaphor.

After her diagnosis with **Multiple Sclerosis (MS)**, Wendy Booker made it her quest to climb the highest mountain on each of the seven continents. Read her blog post on page 69 and then complete the activities below.

📖 Glossary

Multiple Sclerosis (MS)   an inflammatory disease that affects the ability of nerve cells in the brain and spinal cord to communicate with each other effectively

extended metaphor   a metaphor that is repeated or expanded in a text

abstract noun   a noun that refers to a concept, such as 'hope', 'trust', 'pride' or 'determination'

theme   subject or main idea

✎ Activities

1 Why do you think Wendy Booker decided to write this entry on her blog? Think about:

- what she has chosen to write about
- the purpose of her writing
- who her readers might be.

2 Wendy Booker uses the **extended metaphor** of a mountain to describe her disease. At one point she says 'Just like an individual climber facing insurmountable odds, discomfort, fear, trepidations and perseverance, we with MS face this mountain every day.'

What does the writer's use of this extended metaphor tell us about her attitude to her disease?

3 You have been asked to tag this blog post so that people can find it in web searches more easily. Choose five **abstract nouns** that you would use to describe the **theme** of the blog post. **SPAG**

4 Write a blog post about a time when you have faced and overcome a challenge in your own life. Try to create an extended metaphor in your writing.

☑ Progress Check

Swap your writing with a partner. How effective is the extended metaphor they have created? Can you suggest any ways to improve this?

ignite INTERVIEW

'All sports require you to be incredibly driven and single minded.'

Nikki Emerson

Extract from *Then There Were Four*

In 1914 Ernest Shackleton posted a notice 'Looking for willing and able bodied men to go on a perilous journey from which they may never return'. Over a 1000 applied.

In 2002 I answered a similar notice. I was one of a handful of 'applicants' and so began my amazing journey to climb the highest mountain on each of the seven continents. I wasn't a climber. I wasn't an adventurer…

But the call to attempt to go on a perilous journey of which I knew nothing but wanted to learn was too great… And thus began my new life…

My journey was further complicated by the fact that, unlike Shackleton's able-bodied men, in 1998 I had been diagnosed with MS but that above all else was my very personal reason for attempting this mission. I wanted to see if I could climb with and for MS.

Mountaineering is unlike any other sport. It is a very solitary sport and a team effort both at once. The challenge is met by bringing together a clear, responsible decision as to what is the smart thing to do… A poor decision not only affects the individual climber but also puts great risk on the people who must now give their own lives in order to save that person…

It is all about individual choice. Reaching one's personal boundary and recognizing that we have a responsibility to ourselves, those we care about, the people we are climbing with and to our personal mission…

My mission has been to educate, motivate and encourage those facing MS that they too have the ability to take an amazing journey with their disease. They have the personal responsibility to get on a medication to make themselves the best they can possibly be to face the challenges of the mountain ahead. Just like an individual climber facing **insurmountable** odds, discomfort, fear, **trepidations** and **perseverance**, we with MS face this mountain every day. But only within ourselves do we hold the individual decision to push back, reach and recognize our limitations, challenge our hearts, minds and spirit and live a fulfilling life with and for MS. It is not an easy mission but I personally know it is fate that brought us here. Our spirit that will guide us through. And the rewards are like no other.

📖 Glossary

insurmountable   impossible to overcome

trepidations   fears

perseverance   the quality of being able to continue with an action despite setbacks

(5) Making Your Mark

 Objective

Analyse characterization in a first-person narrative.

A **first-person narrative** makes you see the world through one character's eyes. The way they tell the story can help you to understand more about them. The story that begins on page 71 is narrated by Chato, a **Chicano** teenager who lives in a rundown area of Los Angeles. Read the extract on pages 71–73 and then complete the activities below.

📖 Glossary

first-person narrative   a story told from one character's viewpoint, using the pronoun 'I'

Chicano   a Mexican-American

✎ Activities

1 Discuss why you think the author decided to call his story *The Somebody*.

2 What do you learn about Chato from reading this extract? Think about:

- what he says and what he does
- how other characters react to Chato
- his opinions and attitudes and what these suggest about him.

3 How does the author create a distinctive voice for Chato?

Support

Comment on the style of language used and the way the narrator directly addresses the reader.

4 What does the extract suggest to you about what it feels like to be an outsider? Include references to the text in your answer.

Extract from *The Somebody* by Danny Santiago

This is Chato talking, Chato de Shamrock, from the Eastside in old L.A., and I want you to know this is a big day in my life because today I quit school and went to work as a writer. I write on fences or buildings or anything that comes along. I write my name, not the one I got from my father. I want no part of him. I write Chato, which means Catface, because I have a flat nose like a cat. It's a Mexican word because that's what I am, a Mexican, and I'm not ashamed of it. I like that language, too, man. It's way better than English to say what you feel. But German is the best. It's got a real rugged sound, and I'm going to learn to talk it someday.

After Chato I write 'de Shamrock'. That's the street where I live, and it's the name of the gang I belong to, but the others are all gone now. Their families had to move away, except Gorilla is in jail and Blackie joined the Navy because he liked swimming. But I still have our old **arsenal**. It's buried under the chickens, and I dig it up when I get bored. There's tire irons and chains and pick handles with spikes and two zip guns we made and they shoot real bullets but not very straight. In the good old days nobody cared to tangle with us. But now I'm the only one left.

Well, today started off like any other day. The toilet roars like a hot rod taking off. My father coughs and spits about nineteen times and hollers it's six-thirty. So I holler back I'm quitting school. Things hit me like that – sudden.

📖 Glossary

arsenal   a stock of weapons

More to explore

'Don't you want to be a lawyer no more,' he says in Spanish, 'and defend the Mexican people?' My father thinks he is very funny, and next time I make any plans, he's sure not going to hear about it. 'Don't you want to be a doctor,' he says, 'and cut off my leg for nothing someday?' 'How will you support me,' he says, 'when I retire? Or will you marry a rich old woman that owns a pool hall?' 'I'm checking out of this dump! You'll never see me again!'

I hollered in at him, but already he was in the kitchen making a big noise in his coffee. I could be dead and he wouldn't take me serious. So I laid there and waited for him to go off to work. When I woke up again, it was way past eleven. I can sleep forever these days. So I got out of bed and put on clean jeans and my **windbreaker** and combed myself very neat because already I had a feeling this was going to be a big day for me.

I had to wait for breakfast because the baby was sick and throwing up milk on everything. There is always a baby vomiting in my house. When they're born, everybody comes over and says: 'Que cute!' but nobody passes any comments on the dirty way babies act or the dirty way they were made either. Sometimes my mother asks me to hold one for her but it always cries, maybe because I squeeze it a little hard when nobody's looking.

When my mother finally served me, I had to hold my breath, she smelled so bad of babies. I don't care to look at her anymore. Her legs got those dark-blue rivers running all over them. I kept waiting for her to bawl me out about school, but I guess she forgot, or something. So I cut out.

Every time I go out my front door I have to cry for what they've done to old Shamrock Street. It used to be so fine, with solid homes on both sides. Maybe they needed a little paint here and there but they were cozy. Then the S.P. railroad bought up all the land except my father's place cause he was stubborn. They came in with their wrecking bars and their bulldozers. You could hear those houses scream when they ripped them down. So now Shamrock Street is just front walks that lead to a hole in the ground, and piles of busted cement. And Pelon's house and Blackie's are just stacks of old boards waiting to get hauled away. I hope that never happens to your street, man.

🕐 **Extra Time**

Write the next few paragraphs of the story. Think about how you could show more about Chato's character.

6 Standing Out

↻ Objective

Explore how the theme of conformity is presented in two poems.

Many people don't want to conform and instead decide to show their individuality. You have been asked to evaluate the suitability of the poems on page 75 for a poetry anthology with the title *Challenging Conformity*. Read the poems and then complete the activities.

✎ Activities

1 First choose one of the poems to evaluate. Re-read it two or three times, identifying any details that catch your interest or questions that you want to ask about it.

2 Discuss each poem in turn. Make sure you cover the following questions in your discussion.

- What is the poem about?

- Who is the speaker in the poem? What feelings do they show?

- What language choices or techniques has the poet used and why?

- What imagery is used and how does this reflect the meaning of the poem?

- How is the poem structured?

- What would you say the theme of the poem is?

3 Decide which poem you would choose to include in the poetry anthology. Prepare a presentation for the editors of the anthology, explaining how this poem explores the theme of challenging conformity. You should include a reading of the poem as part of your presentation.

'For Heidi With Blue Hair'
by Fleur Adcock

When you dyed your hair blue
(or, at least, ultramarine
for the clipped sides, with a crest
of jet-black spikes on top)
you were sent home from school

because, as the headmistress put it,
although dyed hair was not
specifically forbidden, yours
was, apart from anything else,
not done in the school colours.

Tears in the kitchen, telephone calls
to school from your freedom-loving father:
'She's not a punk in her behaviour;
it's just a style.' (You wiped your eyes,
also not in a school colour.)

'She discussed it with me first –
we checked the rules.' 'And anyway, Dad,
it cost twenty-five dollars.
Tell them it won't wash out –
not even if I wanted to try.'

It would have been unfair to mention
your mother's death, but that
shimmered behind the arguments.
The school had nothing else against you;
the teachers twittered and gave in.

Next day your black friend had hers done
in grey, white and flaxen yellow –
the school colours precisely:
an act of solidarity, a witty
tease. The battle was already won.

'Warning'
by Jenny Joseph

When I am an old woman I shall wear purple
With a red hat which doesn't go, and doesn't suit me.
And I shall spend my pension on brandy and summer gloves
And satin sandals, and say we've no money for butter.
I shall sit down on the pavement when I'm tired
And gobble up samples in shops and press alarm bells
And run my stick along the public railings
And make up for the sobriety of my youth.
I shall go out in my slippers in the rain
And pick flowers in other people's gardens
And learn to spit.

You can wear terrible shirts and grow more fat
And eat three pounds of sausages at a go
Or only bread and pickle for a week
And hoard pens and pencils and beermats and things in boxes.

But now we must have clothes that keep us dry
And pay our rent and not swear in the street
And set a good example for the children.
We must have friends to dinner and read the papers.

But maybe I ought to practise a little now?
So people who know me are not too shocked and surprised
When suddenly I am old, and start to wear purple.

7 The Outsider

↻ Objective

Explore characterization in a pre-1914 literary heritage novel.

Fiction has the power to bring characters to life. Writers depict these characters in detail, conveying their physical appearances, personalities, behaviours and conditions. The extract on page 77 is taken from George Eliot's novel *Silas Marner*, in which Silas, a weaver, lives as an outcast. In this extract, taken from Chapter 1 of the novel, we are introduced to Silas and the community of Raveloe. Read the extract and then complete the activities.

✎ Activities

1 In pairs or small groups discuss your initial reaction to this extract, which was written by George Eliot as one paragraph. Explain to one another what you think is happening in the extract. Look up any words that you don't understand either in the glossary opposite or in a dictionary.

2a Working on your own, now look at the text more closely. Write an answer to each of the following questions, making use of quotations or examples where you can.

How is Silas Marner described in the opening sentence?

2b Where do you think 'North'ard' is?

2c Looking at the extract as a whole, what is it about Silas that seems to isolate him from the villagers?

2d At the end of the extract, why does Mr Macey believe that Silas is not suffering a fit or a stroke?

2e Silas Marner suffers from **catalepsy**. How does knowing this alter your view of Silas and your view of the villagers?

3 What do we learn about Silas Marner and the villagers from this extract? Copy and complete the grid below, aiming to find at least four pieces of evidence for Silas Marner and at least three for the villagers. An example has been provided for you.

Character	Evidence	What this might tell us
Silas Marner	Eyes 'set like a dead man's'	He's tired, ill or wrapped up in his own thoughts.
The villagers		

Extract from *Silas Marner* by George Eliot

It was fifteen years since Silas Marner had first come to Raveloe; he was then simply a **pallid** young man, with prominent short-sighted brown eyes, whose appearance would have had nothing strange for people of average culture and experience, but for the villagers near whom he had come to settle it had mysterious peculiarities which corresponded with the exceptional nature of his occupation, and his advent from an unknown region called 'North'ard'. So had his way of life:–he invited no comer to step across his door-sill, and he never strolled into the village to drink a pint at the Rainbow, or to gossip at the **wheelwright's**: he sought no man or woman, save for the purposes of his calling, or in order to supply himself with necessaries; and it was soon clear to the Raveloe lasses that he would never urge one of them to accept him against her will–quite as if he had heard them declare that they would never marry a dead man come to life again. This view of Marner's personality was not without another ground than his pale face and unexampled eyes; for Jem Rodney, the mole-catcher, averred that one evening as he was returning homeward, he saw Silas Marner leaning against a stile with a heavy bag on his back, instead of resting the bag on the stile as a man in his senses would have done; and that, on coming up to him, he saw that Marner's eyes were set like a dead man's, and he spoke to him, and shook him, and his limbs were stiff, and his hands clutched the bag as if they'd been made of iron; but just as he had made up his mind that the weaver was dead, he came all right again, like, as you might say, in the winking of an eye, and said 'Good-night', and walked off. All this Jem swore he had seen, more by token that it was the very day he had been mole-catching on Squire Cass's land, down by the old saw-pit. Some said Marner must have been in a 'fit', a word which seemed to explain things otherwise incredible; but the argumentative Mr. Macey, clerk of the parish, shook his head, and asked if anybody was ever known to go off in a fit and not fall down. A fit was a **stroke**, wasn't it? and it was in the nature of a stroke to partly take away the use of a man's limbs and throw him on the parish, if he'd got no children to look to. No, no; it was no stroke that would let a man stand on his legs, like a horse between the shafts, and then walk off as soon as you can say 'Gee!'

📖 Glossary

catalepsy a medical condition where the body becomes stiff and the person becomes temporarily unconscious

pallid pale

wheelwright someone who builds or repairs wooden wheels

stroke paralysis in the body caused by an interruption in the blood flow to the brain

🕐 Extra Time

What was life in the village of Raveloe like for Silas Marner? Write two or three paragraphs from his perspective, based on what you have learned from this extract.

8 Assessment:
Reading Analysis of an Extract from *Lord of the Flies*

In English Literature exams, for example at GCSE, students are expected to write an essay in response to a novel or an extract from a novel. You are now going to read an extract from the novel *Lord of the Flies* by William Golding. The novel is about a group of boys from different schools and backgrounds who are stranded on an isolated island after a plane crash. In the extract that begins on page 80, two of the boys, Ralph and Piggy, meet for the first time.

Use the skills you have developed throughout this unit to write an essay answering the following question:

How does Golding show the differences between the characters of Ralph and Piggy?

In your answer you should comment on:

* the characterization of the two boys

* how language and linguistic devices are used to convey meaning

* the way the extract is structured.

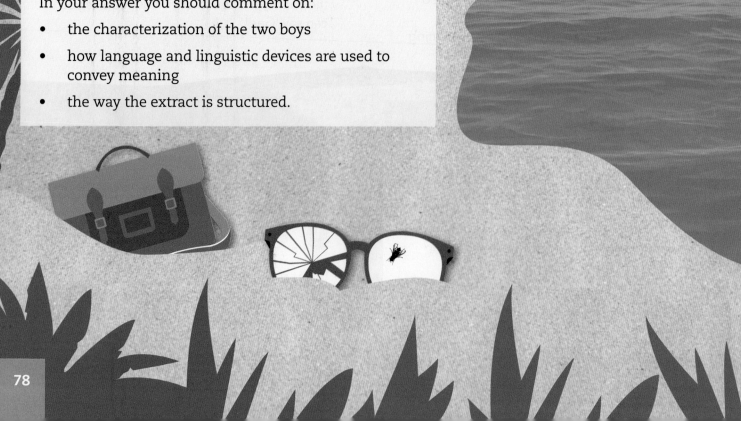

Before you write...

Think about the question as you read the extract. Make notes of any details that you think might be helpful to refer to when you answer the question. Then consider the questions below as you re-read the extract.

- What do we learn about the two boys?

- What contrasts are made between them?

- How do they react to being stranded on the island?

- What can you tell about their relationship?

As you write...

Write an essay answering the question: **How does Golding show the differences between the characters of Ralph and Piggy?** Remember that for an essay, you will need to:

- use Standard English

- refer to evidence and quotations from the text

- start with an introductory paragraph

- group your ideas into separate paragraphs

- finish with a clear conclusion.

Note that for the purposes of this assessment, you will be marked on your reading and analysis skills, rather than on your writing skills.

More to explore

Extract from *Lord of the Flies* by William Golding

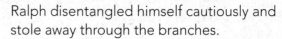

'What's your name?'

'Ralph.'

The fat boy waited to be asked his name in turn but this **proffer** of acquaintance was not made; the fair boy called Ralph smiled vaguely, stood up, and began to make his way once more toward the lagoon. The fat boy hung steadily at his shoulder.

'I expect there's a lot more of us scattered about. You haven't seen any others, have you?'

Ralph shook his head and increased his speed. Then he tripped over a branch and came down with a crash.

The fat boy stood by him, breathing hard.

'My auntie told me not to run,' he explained, 'on account of my asthma.'

'Ass-mar?'

'That's right. Can't catch me breath. I was the only boy in our school what had asthma,' said the fat boy with a touch of pride. 'And I've been wearing specs since I was three.'

He took off his glasses and held them out to Ralph, blinking and smiling, and then started to wipe them against his grubby windbreaker. An expression of pain and inward concentration altered the pale **contours** of his face. He smeared the sweat from his cheeks and quickly adjusted the spectacles on his nose.

'Them fruit.'

He glanced round the **scar**.

'Them fruit,' he said, 'I expect —'

He put on his glasses, waded away from Ralph, and crouched down among the tangled foliage.

'I'll be out again in just a minute —'

Ralph disentangled himself cautiously and stole away through the branches.

In a few seconds the fat boy's grunts were behind him and he was hurrying towards the screen that still lay between him and the lagoon. He climbed over a broken trunk and was out of the jungle.

The shore was fledged with palm trees. These stood or leaned or reclined against the light and their green feathers were a hundred feet up in the air. The ground beneath them was a bank covered with coarse grass, torn everywhere by the upheavals of fallen trees, scattered with decaying coco-nuts and palm saplings. Behind this was the darkness of the forest proper and the open space of the scar. Ralph stood, one hand against a grey trunk, and screwed up his eyes against the shimmering water. Out there, perhaps a mile away, the white surf flinked on a coral reef, and beyond that the open sea was dark blue. Within the irregular arc of coral the lagoon was still as a mountain lake — blue of all shades and shadowy green and purple. The beach between the palm terrace and the water was a thin bow-stave, endless apparently, for to Ralph's left the perspectives of palm and beach and water drew to a point at infinity; and always, almost visible, was the heat.

📖 Glossary

proffer   offer

contours   outline, like the lines on a map that show the shape and height of a landscape

scar   as the aeroplane crashed on the island it tore a path through the jungle. Golding describes this as a 'scar'.

He jumped down from the terrace. The sand was thick over his black shoes and the heat hit him. He became conscious of the weight of clothes, kicked his shoes off fiercely and ripped off each stocking with its elastic garter in a single movement. Then he leapt back on the terrace, pulled off his shirt, and stood there among the skull-like coco-nuts with green shadows from the palms and the forest sliding over his skin. He undid the snake-clasp of his belt, lugged off his shorts and pants, and stood there naked, looking at the dazzling beach and the water.

He was old enough, twelve years and a few months, to have lost the prominent tummy of childhood; and not yet old enough for adolescence to have made him awkward. You could see now that he might make a boxer, as far as width and heaviness of shoulders went, but there was a mildness about his mouth and eyes that proclaimed no devil. He patted the palm trunk softly; and, forced at last to believe in the reality of the island, laughed delightedly again and stood on his head. He turned neatly on to his feet, jumped down to the beach, knelt and swept a double armful of sand into a pile against his chest. Then he sat back and looked at the water with bright, excited eyes.

'Ralph —'

The fat boy lowered himself over the terrace and sat down carefully, using the edge as a seat.

'I'm sorry I been such a time. Them fruit —'

He wiped his glasses and adjusted them on his button nose. The frame had made a deep, pink 'V' on the bridge. He looked critically at Ralph's golden body and then down at his own clothes. He laid a hand on the end of a zipper that extended down his chest.

'My auntie —'

Then he opened the zipper with decision and pulled the whole windbreaker over his head.

'There!'

Ralph looked at him side-long and said nothing.

'I expect we'll want to know all their names,' said the fat boy, 'and make a list. We ought to have a meeting.'

Ralph did not take the hint so the fat boy was forced to continue.

'I don't care what they call me,' he said confidentially, 'so long as they don't call me what they used to call me at school.'

Ralph was faintly interested.

'What was that?'

The fat boy glanced over his shoulder, then leaned toward Ralph.

He whispered.

'They used to call me "Piggy".'

Ralph shrieked with laughter. He jumped up.

'Piggy! Piggy!'

'Ralph — please!'

Piggy clasped his hands in apprehension.

'I said I didn't want —'

'Piggy! Piggy!'

Ralph danced out into the hot air of the beach and then returned as a fighter-plane, with wings swept back, and machine-gunned Piggy.

4

I declare after all there is no enjoyment like reading.
~ Jane Austen

SHOPPING

WAS £29.99
NOW £2.99

My LifE

my Choices

What matters to you?

SK8

DON'T FORGET TO PRACTISE

THE OXFORD EAGLES
BASKETBALL CLUB

Only £29

PERFECT PARTY DRE

Introduction

As you grow up you have more choices to make, such as where you go, how you look, what you buy, and what you do with your free time. So how do you make those choices? What influences you?

This unit explores those choices and influences through a variety of non-fiction texts, such as feature articles in magazines, newspapers or websites, blogs, petitions, reviews and reports. At the end of the unit, you will write your own feature for a teen website about something that interests and matters to you.

ignite INTERVIEW
Lisa Sewards, Feature writer

Feature writing tends to be an interview or an in-depth look at a subject or a person. People read features because they want to learn something new. At the forefront of your mind you always have your audience, the reason to interview somebody and what you need to get out of an interview. The key ingredient for every feature is to say something new if you can or, if it is saying something that has been written before, to say it in a different way. Pick out the most interesting material that is relevant to your readership and use quotations to add something extra.

Activities

1 You are part of a focus group for a new magazine designed for young people. What do you think it should contain? Think about:

- ideas for feature articles
- the mix of information and entertainment
- how to let your readers have their say.

Record your ideas in the form of a spider diagram. Use your diagram to create a contents page for the magazine.

1 Have Your Say

↻ Objective

Discuss an issue and prepare a presentation to convey a viewpoint.

Where do you meet your friends outside school? Is there much choice in your local area? This is an issue that concerns many young people and the communities in which they live. Read the extracts on page 85 and complete the activities below.

📖 Glossary

rhetorical question a question asked for effect that doesn't require an answer

✎ Activities

1 What might the 'source of tension' referred to in the first extract lead to? What do you think 'anti-social behaviour' refers to in the second extract?

2 Do you think the council's ideas for Ham are worthwhile? Why or why not?

3 Talk about the facilities in your local area for your age group.

- Draw up a list of positive and negative aspects of what is available.
- Suggest an additional local facility you would like to see provided for young people.

4 Plan a three-minute presentation about what you believe your local area offers young people and how these facilities could be improved or added to.

📚 Support

Make notes in two sections: 'Existing facilities' and 'Improvements or additions'. Use bullet points to list your ideas.

↔ Stretch

Plan how to make your presentation as persuasive as possible, using rhetorical techniques such as **rhetorical questions**, repetition, emphasizing key words, using pauses for impact, varying pace and intonation.

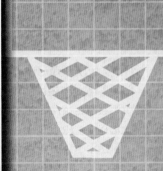

Extract 1
from a Local Community Action Plan
for Netherne on the Hill

Lack of facilities for young people

Residents expressed concern about provision for young people, through interviews, questionnaire responses and feedback sessions. It was stated that:

- Village plans for Netherne on the Hill show facilities for younger children and adults, but none for teenagers.

- Teenagers have few dedicated facilities now and tend to depend on their parents for transport.

- Young people are using communal paved areas for skateboarding and ball games. This is a matter of concern to some residents.

- This is a potential source of tension between different sections of the community.

Extract 2
from the London Borough of Richmond Upon Thames website

Council considers new games area for young people in Ham

Richmond Council is aiming to consider proposals for a new games area for local young people in Ham at a planning meeting on 6 September.

The new multi-use games area, which is planned for the area behind the Ham and Petersham Youth Club in Ham Close, will include a new sealed court area suitable for football and basketball. It will also be fitted with floodlights and will be open until 9pm on weeknights…

Councillor Christine Percival, Richmond Council's Strategic Cabinet Member for Education, Youth and Children's Services, said:

'The new games area proposed for Ham will ensure a safe and well-equipped environment for our youngsters to meet their friends, get plenty of exercise, try out new sports and develop their team-building skills.

Boredom and a lack of facilities are often the root causes of anti-social behaviour and youth violence in our community, so one of our key priorities is to provide local young people with appropriate spaces where they can spend their spare time in a positive way.'

2 Getting What You Want

↺ Objective

Explore the use of persuasive devices in a campaign text.

How would you campaign for better local facilities for young people? Online petitions are becoming increasingly popular. Read the one below, which lobbies for more after-school clubs for primary school children.

The lack of after-school provision in Dealton is a major problem for parents and carers. Only one nursery offers an after-school club. Pupils have to be collected from school and face a significant walk, often in the cold and the wet, in order to attend. How are working parents supposed to manage? How many people finish work at 3pm?

The government says it wants to support people who work and yet there is no reliable after-school care for our children. Unless you have extended family, exceptionally kind neighbours or another parent with whom to share the load, juggling work and childcare can become a nightmare. Between 9am and 3pm, the school gates are locked and the entry phone system ensures that our children are protected; but what about between 3pm and the time that most people finish work? How can the safety and well-being of vulnerable children be allocated a time slot?

The solution is to provide an after-school club within school. This would ensure that children remain safe and parents could work until a reasonable time. If the school permitted this, parents who don't work could earn some extra income by supervising the club and subsidies would not need to be high.

If you believe that this is an important issue, whether you work or not, please sign this petition so that, together, we can start to put pressure on our local head teacher and the local authority to make after-school provision a reality.

SIGN HERE

Activities

1 Most petitions follow a clear structure.

- The problem is set out.
- A solution is proposed.
- A request is made to support the action/solution.

Decide whether the petition on page 86 follows this structure. Be prepared to explain its structure.

2 Find examples of at least four of the following persuasive devices in the petition, and explain their effect.

> Rhetorical questions

> Repetition of key words and phrases

> Patterns of three

> Specific examples

> Emotive language

> Use of first-person plural ('we')

3 Write an online petition to **lobby** your local council for better youth facilities. Include some specific suggestions, such as regenerating a disused building for a youth club, constructing a skate park, or finding premises for a pop-up café.

Support

Remember to structure your petition carefully and to use persuasive devices.

Glossary

emotive language words used to create an emotional response

lobby try to persuade an important person to support your cause

Progress Check

Swap the first draft of your petition with a partner and proofread each other's work. Check for:

- accurate spelling and punctuation
- a clear, logical structure
- effective use of persuasive devices.

Extra Time

Write a formal letter from the council Recreation Sub-Committee in response to your petition.

3 A Sporting Chance

↻ Objective

Explore how writers present arguments and counter-arguments.

How do you choose to stay fit and healthy? Many people take part in sports and benefit from the physical exercise, as well as enjoying the social aspects. There is a huge variety of sports to choose from.

✎ Activities

1 Make a list of sports that you think are competitive and another list of sports or fitness activities that are **non-competitive**. Which do you prefer and why?

2a Read the source text on the right. How does the imagery make the text more entertaining?

2b Why do you think the writer prefers the non-competitive approach?

📖 Glossary

non-competitive not competing against other people

Flying Scotsman famous steam train that ran between Edinburgh and London

Extract from
The World According to Clarkson
by Jeremy Clarkson

My eldest daughter is not sleek. In fact, to be brutally honest she has the aerodynamic properties of a bungalow...

She puts a huge effort into running. Her arms and legs flail around like the **Flying Scotsman's** pistons…

Luckily, the school tries to operate a strict 'no competition' rule. The game starts, children exert energy and then the game finishes. This doesn't work terribly well with the 50-metre running race but often there are never any winners and consequently there are never any losers.

3a Read the extract on the right. What arguments does the writer put forward for competitive sport?

3b How does the writer counter the argument that competitive sport can lower self-esteem?

4 A sports magazine wants to publish readers' views about competitive and non-competitive sports. Write a letter or email weighing up the pros and cons of competitive sports and then give your personal opinion. Start your letter or email, 'Dear Editor…'

Support

Use the following paragraph structure:

- Opening – introduce your subject.
- Argument in favour – present the positive aspects of competitive sports.
- Argument against – outline the negative aspects of competitive sports.
- Conclusion – finish with a well-considered opinion.

Extract from 'A Manifesto for the Reintroduction of Competition in Schools' by Dan Travis

We should bring back sports days with meaningful, traditional sports, and end meaningless team 'participation games' involving parachutes or sponges. Let's have a race and take pride in the best runners, jumpers and throwers. Let's reward children and bring back prize-giving, certificates and trophies. We should make it a mission to help fund and maintain weekly competitions within and between schools…

Competitive sport can temporarily lower self-esteem if you lose and raise it if you win. But let it be known that a temporary loss of self-esteem will not cause permanent damage to children. We should challenge the notion of 'inclusivity' whenever it is used to tamper with competitive sports. We need to let the kids get on with the match, and learn to deal with success and failure and treat those two impostors just the same.

Extra Time

Your school has been given funds for a new after-school fitness club. Write the text for a leaflet or poster advertising this new club.

4 Parental Pressure

↺ Objectives

- Evaluate the effect of expert opinion and statistical information.

- Explore emotive language.

DON'T FORGET TO PRACTISE

As we grow up, we have to make our own choices. Sometimes we want the same things as the adults who care for us, but at other times we have to find our own way and stand up for what we want.

NEWS VOICES | SPORT | TECH | LIFE | PROPERTY | ARTS & ENTS | TRAVEL

UK | WORLD | BUSINESS | PEOPLE | SCIENCE | ENVIRONMENT | MEDIA | TECHNOLOGY | EDUCATION

PUSHY PARENTS
'CHASING LOST DREAMS'

It is what many a child forced to endure endless tennis, piano and acting lessons has long suspected.

Pushy parents who go to great lengths to make their children succeed are attempting to make up for their own failed dreams, say psychologists…

'Some parents see their children as extensions of themselves, rather than as separate people with their own hopes and dreams,' said study co-author Professor Brad Bushman, of Ohio State University.

'These parents may be most likely to want their children to achieve the dreams that they themselves have not achieved.'…

The theory could hold some truth for Andy Murray, whose tennis career has eclipsed that of his mother.

After coaching him during the early stages of his career, Judy Murray – a former professional player – is often filmed egging her son on and celebrating his victories from the sidelines.

The study… was carried out at Utrecht University in the Netherlands.

Eight fathers and 65 mothers of children aged between eight and 15 were asked to complete a test to measure how much they saw their child as a part of themselves.

Parents who felt strongly that they did were more likely to want their offspring to fulfil their own lost dreams, such as writing a novel or starting a successful business.

Professor Bushman added: 'Parents then may bask in the reflected glory of their children, and lose some of the feelings of regret and disappointment that they couldn't achieve these same goals.'

✎ Activities

1a Read the newspaper extract on page 90, which reports on a study. What effect do the quotations from the experts involved have on the reader? What do the reported statistics add to the article?

1b Identify five emotive words or phrases. What kinds of reactions do these create in the reader?

1c How does the Andy Murray anecdote help to illustrate the point of the article?

1d Write a headline for this article, including one of the emotive words that you identified in the article. Explain why your headline would catch the reader's attention.

ignite INTERVIEW

'Include facts and figures in the feature to set the scene and use quotations to add something extra.'

Lisa Sewards

My Mum wants me to have a career that I don't want

It breaks my heart listening to people at my school picking their A levels and hearing that they have support from their parents. My Mum is quite traditional and thinks that I should work in medicine. She has chosen my A levels: biology, chemistry and maths.

I would choose English literature, art and musical theatre, as I would love to be a performer.

2 Read the letter above. Write the script for a scene in which this young person decides to stand up to his or her mother. The scene could be used at Options events to encourage parental support for their children's own choices. Make sure you include some emotive language.

Support

You could use the script below to start your scene:

Mrs Attawar   I hope you chose biology, chemistry and maths as your options, like we discussed.

Nadir   Well, actually, I wanted to talk to you about that. You see…

Stretch

Write a short speech for a teacher to introduce and explain the purpose of the scene at the Options evening.

5 Fashion Victims

↻ Objective

Understand how writers use language to engage the reader.

We all choose how we look, to some extent. What we choose is a statement about ourselves, even if that statement is, 'I don't care how I look!'

✎ Activities

1 Name and describe as many different fashion trends as you can. Use the images on this page to help you.

↔ Stretch

Think carefully about what messages these fashions send out. What do they suggest about the person wearing them?

ignite INTERVIEW

'The key ingredient for every feature is to say something new if you can or, if it is saying something that has been written before, to say it in a different way.'

Lisa Sewards

Fashion is nothing new. Read the extract below. It is from a blog by a writer of historical fiction.

Macaroni! And I Don't Mean Pasta

Every era has its extremes of dress. The Sixties had micro-minis. The Roaring Twenties had flapper dresses. Georgian England had **macaronis**…

Brought from the continent by idle young men on their Grand Tour, macaroni dress took the standard male wardrobe of wig, coat, waistcoat, breeches, stockings and shoes to absurd lengths. The express purpose was to shock people. And shock they did. Coats were tight. Huge buttons decorated short waistcoats. Narrow, dainty shoes sported buckles almost larger than they were. And copious amounts of lace, ribbon, ruffles and whatever other outrageous decoration took the wearer's fancy trimmed the outfits, with everything in gaudy colours and showy fabrics like silks and satins.

Perhaps the most obvious feature of macaroni fashion was the wig… macaroni wigs were excessively elaborate and tall, and, by contrast, crowned with a tiny hat that literally could be removed only with the point of a sword…

The Macaroni Penguin, a large crested penguin native to Antarctica and the southern tip of South America, owes its name to the Georgian macaronis. English mariners in the Falkland Islands, off the coast of Chile, named the bird. With its flamboyant, coloured head feathers, the penguin reminded the sailors of the macaronis back home.

2a Why do you think these fashionable young men were called 'macaronis'?

2b What vocabulary does the writer use to emphasize how extreme the macaroni fashion was?

2c How does the writer use language to engage the reader? Think about:

- the rule of three
- variation in sentence length
- detailed description
- humorous imagery.

SPAG

3 Write a short description of a fashion trend for an online magazine. It can be an old or a current trend. Try to use language devices that will engage your reader.

📖 Glossary

macaronis   young, rich men who wore an extreme fashion style in the mid-1700s

6 Cheapskates

↻ Objective

Use talk and role-play to explore complex issues.

We all make choices about what we wear, but is this choice all about how we want to look or should it also be about what is morally right? In recent years, more information has become available about how our clothes are made. This has led to new trends such as ethical clothing and upcycling.

✎ Activities

1 Read the newspaper article on page 95. If you were part of the editorial team on a rival newspaper, how would you cover this story? In groups, discuss:

- what **angle** you might take

- who you would interview to get a range of viewpoints

- what questions you would ask at the interviews.

2 Role-play your interviews and make a note of key quotations that you would use in your article.

3 Make a first draft of your article. Try to explore the issue from different viewpoints, using ideas that emerged in the interviews.

ignite INTERVIEW

'Type up the interview and sift through the most relevant information or the most fascinating part of the interview and then start the introduction with that. Put the most interesting facts and the most interesting things you think you might want to read about at the top of the feature and then work down to the less interesting information. This is what we call a 'triangle'.'

Lisa Sewards

📖 Glossary

angle   the point or theme of a news or feature story

☑ Progress Check

Exchange your draft with a partner. Highlight two strong aspects of each other's draft and suggest one area that could be improved.

PRIMARK AND THE HIGH STREET

WHY ARE THE WORKERS WHO MAKE OUR CHEAP CLOTHES PAYING WITH THEIR LIVES?

Campaign groups around the world are rightly rounding on Primark following the tragic collapse of one of their suppliers' factories in Bangladesh last week which, at the last count, killed nearly 300 people.

Labels from a number of the UK's most popular – and profitable – High Street brands… were found amongst the rubble.

But is Primark, with its cheap-as-chips, stack-'em-high sales pitch really the worst of the bunch when it comes to workers' rights?

Sadly not.

The recent factory collapse is only the latest of many such incidents which happen every year in Bangladesh and other major garment-producing countries around the world. These incidents happen depressingly often due to a lack of health and safety regulations such as blocked fire escapes and lack of ventilation…

So why are the workers who make our cheap clothes still paying with their lives?

The answer lies in the way that the global garment industry operates which allows companies to evade their responsibility for the often appalling sweatshop working conditions at these factories…

So if you want to avoid ethically dodgy High Street stores who should you avoid?

The bad news is that unpicking the threads of this issue is eye-wateringly complicated simply

because it's virtually impossible to establish what clothes were made in what factory and whether the workers there are being paid a fair wage…

So much for the bad news.

The good news is that here in the UK we have a thriving ethical fashion sector which is proving that your shirts and skirts can be produced without putting workers' lives at risk.

In the latest Ethical Consumer Product Guide to fashion we've named over a dozen Best Buy ethical clothing companies… who are forging an entirely new business model for the clothing industry, one based on generating a market for artisan clothing from around the world rather than ripping-off workers…

My challenge to everyone is to halve the quantity of clothes you buy and double your spend on each item. Use your money wisely and you can stop supporting the sweatshop-producers…

Something as frivolous as fashion shouldn't be a life and death issue.

7 Branding: Slavery or Loyalty?

↻ Objective

Identify attitudes and beliefs conveyed within texts.

Whenever you buy something, you make a choice, but what influences that choice? Many people choose to buy branded goods. They see it as a loyalty to a label that guarantees quality. Other people believe that following a brand is a form of slavery promoted by companies who want to own the market and the consumer.

✎ Activities

1 Read the quotation below from BrandPie, a company that helps businesses to develop their own brand. List three brands you feel a loyalty to. Do you believe they do what BrandPie recommends? Explain your answer.

Strong brands know what they represent. They have a distinctive visual identity and tone of voice. They speak clearly to people in words and images.

2a Read the quotation on the right from Will.i.am about the word 'consumer'.

Why does Will.i.am choose to use the word 'champion'? What does this word suggest about his attitude?

2b How does Will.i.am's statement aim to make the reader feel?

Forget the Consumer

'"Consumer" is a bad name to call people. Tomorrow the word looks more like "champion". People have to champion your brand, not just consume. They add value, making you relevant. Calling them consumers undermines their power. And they can also destroy you. "Brand" is a bad word too. It's your company. Because brand is associated with branding. People aren't cattle.'

Will.i.am

3a Now read the report on page 97. Find evidence in the report which supports Will.i.am's belief in the power of the consumer.

3b Which words and phrases suggest that the writer of this report believes Apple is a worthy winner of the award?

3c How does he ensure that his beliefs seem well-considered?

3d Explain the meaning of the words 'revolutionizing', 'aesthetics' and 'iconic'. If they are unfamiliar use the context or your knowledge of similar words to work out their meaning, before checking in a dictionary.

3e Summarize the text in 50 words or fewer.

Extract from 'Interbrand Best Global Brands 2013 Report' by Jez Frampton

Every so often, a company changes our lives, not just with its products, but with its ethos. This is why, following Coca-Cola's 13-year run at the top of Best Global Brands, Interbrand has a new #1—Apple. Few brands have enabled so many people to do so much so easily, which is why Apple has legions of adoring fans. For revolutionizing the way we work, play, and communicate— and for mastering the ability to surprise and delight—Apple has set a high bar for aesthetics, simplicity, and ease of use that all other tech brands are now expected to match, and that Apple itself is expected to continually exceed. . .

With the customer at the **nexus** of everything it does, Apple continues to respond to emerging needs, improve its products, and break new ground in design and performance.

Living up to the brand's iconic 'Think Different' campaign, Apple's designers and engineers reimagined the operating system that powers the iPhone, iPad, and iPod touch. Incorporating a more sophisticated tool to help protect users' data and discourage theft, iOS 7's innovative new features include an activation lock, which prevents a stolen phone from being re-activated, even if a device is wiped…

The company has announced that the Mac Pro will be assembled in the US, which demonstrates that Apple has taken criticism over Foxconn worker conditions in China to heart. The brand's environmental commitments also appear to be growing.

However, its reputation has taken a few hits this past year, including being found guilty by a US court of conspiring with publishers to fix the price of e-books bought via iTunes; the ongoing Apple vs. Samsung patent trials; allegations around treatment of workers at a supplier (Foxconn) in China; and a US Senate hearing examining the company's 'highly questionable' tax minimization strategies. On the plus side, a portfolio of blockbuster products, promising upgrades, and new and improved services are sure to remind users—and investors—what they love about Apple...

Whether that innovation turns out to be the iWatch or something completely unexpected, it's Apple's ability to 'think different'— truly different—and to deeply consider our needs that will keep it on, or near, the top for years to come.

---

4 Read the following quotations. Decide whether you agree or disagree with each and explain your opinions.

> I buy a brand because it tells me what to expect. It stands for consistency and quality.

> Any company that puts their brand name on the outside of clothes doesn't get my business. I don't desire to be a walking billboard.

📖 Glossary

nexus   means of connection; a hub or link

8 You Are What You Tweet

↺ Objective

Understand the effect of structural and grammatical devices in an article.

How do you choose to portray yourself online? With the increasing use of social media, more people are creating profiles, sharing photographs, opinions, jokes and information than ever before. Such easy communication has many advantages, but it also has its dangers.

Read the extract on page 99 and complete the activities below.

📖 Glossary

personal pronouns first-person pronouns refer to the speaker ('I' or 'we'); second-person pronouns refer to the person being addressed ('you'); third-person pronouns refer to third parties other than the speaker or the person being addressed ('he', 'she', 'it', 'they')

imperative form of verb that is like a command, usually found at the start of a sentence, e.g. *Look…, Make…, Go…*

✎ Activities

1 Think about the original meanings of the words 'tweet' and 'twitter'. Why do you think they have become synonymous with social networking?

2 Read the heading and subheadings. How do they engage the reader and help to structure the article?

3 What **personal pronouns** does the writer predominantly use? How do they influence the tone of the article and its effect on the reader? **SPAG**

4 The writer uses two **imperatives** when giving advice in the final couple of paragraphs of the text. What are they? Why does he use the imperative form? **SPAG**

5 Write a short advice text for someone new to social networking (perhaps a younger sibling). Think carefully about how best to present and structure the advice for your audience.

You Are What You Tweet: How Social Media Define Our Professional Brands

I cannot help but wonder what pictures, tweets and videos our future presidential candidates and business leaders are currently posting. And if they're even thinking about what those images and words will say about them. Are they relying on the discretion of their 'friends,' 'fans' or 'followers'?...

The Internet Is Forever

Sometimes we think better of something we have said or posted and we hit 'delete'. But gone is not gone on the Internet. Even when your original tweet is gone, for example, the retweets continue to live on, with your username attached...

Pictures you posted of your last vacation may show up in places you never expected, as people search Google for images. Depending on where you work, that small bathing suit that is perfectly appropriate on the beaches of the Caribbean might not be the image you want your colleagues, co-workers or supervisor seeing.

That means, as much as you'd like to recall that message, or remove that posting, it may be too late. Even if your privacy settings are the most restricted available, are you sure that all of your Facebook friends have done the same?...

Don't Panic

Of course, it is not time to throw away all of our devices and give up on social media. Rather, take advantage of the tremendous opportunity for personal branding that social media represent. All that is required in this new interconnected world is a certain level of understanding and the appropriate preparation.

Don't put things online that you wouldn't be comfortable seeing again one day. This may be a particularly hard lesson for people who have not entered the professional world, but hope to one day. They've grown up with technology as a trusted means of self-expression.

9 Read All About It

↺ Objective

Explore how fact and opinion are combined in a review.

Most of us start to connect with music and songs when we are very young, but as we grow up we explore a wider range of music and are usually drawn to some types of music more than others. Reviews help us to find out more about the artists and songs that appeal to us and help us choose what music to purchase.

✎ Activities

1 List four music tracks you would take with you to a desert island and explain why you chose them.

2a Read the review of Bob Marley's album, 'Songs of Freedom', on page 101. List the facts you can deduce from this review. (Remember that facts can be proven.)

2b Choose two adjectives that show the strength of the writer's personal opinion about Marley's music. Explain the meaning and **connotations** of those adjectives.

SPAG

2c Which sentence do you think best sums up the reviewer's opinion of Marley's music? Explain your choice.

2d What effect does this review have on you in terms of your knowledge and attitude to Bob Marley's music?

📖 Glossary

connotations ideas or feelings that a word triggers, in addition to its main, literal meaning

REVIEW OF
BOB MARLEY'S 'SONGS OF FREEDOM'

Bob Marley was a genius: an inventive and extraordinary musician, a honeyed singer, a songwriter of mystic power, and a statesman of revolutionary proportions. His achievements stand side by side with those of The Beatles, Elvis, James Brown and Marvin Gaye. He was the Third World's first (and possibly last) worldwide superstar. He was the man.

Previously, those unfamiliar with Marley could only find out about his musical prowess by either buying his dozen or so albums or the 'Legend' compilation, as millions of others have. 'Songs Of Freedom', however, bridges that gap and includes four CDs which chart the whole of Marley's musical life.

'Songs Of Freedom' demonstrates how Marley combined fierce, rebellious lyrics with lovely, moving melodies. It tells the story of how the son of a British army captain and a teenage Jamaican girl grew up in one of Jamaica's toughest ghettos and brought reggae music to an international audience. This compilation includes material from each of his studio albums, as well as rare versions, B-sides, outtakes, and live recordings.

While 78 songs do not seem quite comprehensive enough, we must remember that Marley was only 36 when he died. The superstar who united Jamaica's politicians and brought reggae to the world was struck down by a toe injury that turned cancerous.

Such an end seems ridiculous for this great man, but maybe the redemptive power of Marley's music was too much for this world. That music, though, pure and sweet and powerful, continues to perform miracles to this day.

More to explore

Activities continued

3a Read the review of an Emeli Sandé gig on page 103. How does the writer weave fact and opinion together in the first paragraph?

3b The article contains a number of informal words. Select three of these and explain what they add to the article.

Support

Think about audience and purpose when considering the effect of these informal words.

3c The article uses several **metaphors**. Identify one metaphor and explain how it conveys the writer's opinion effectively.

3d The writer uses the word 'disser'. Think about what the prefix dis- means and reflect on the context of the word, and then write a definition of the word 'disser'.

SPAG

4 Think of a musical artist whom you admire. Write a short review of their life, an album or a famous track they have released. Aim to include a mixture of fact and opinion and include some acceptable informal words and phrases.

ignite INTERVIEW

'In feature writing, at the forefront of your mind you always have your audience.'

Lisa Sewards

Glossary

metaphor describing something as something else, not meant to be taken literally, e.g. *You are a star.*

ubiquity capacity to be everywhere at the same time

vim enthusiasm

debutant somebody making a debut or first appearance

valedictory farewell

conundrum puzzle

Extra Time

Plan the vocabulary for a tag cloud (word cloud) on the website of a musician of your choice.

EMELI SANDÉ—LIVE

There was some confusion organizing this review of Emeli Sandé's run of gigs at London's Hammersmith Apollo. For a short time her label's PR department seemed endearingly unaware that the Scottish singer was playing three consecutive nights at the 5,000-plus capacity venue, not two. 'Of course it's three nights,' I wanted to reply, 'it's Emeli Sandé.'

There is always more Sandé on offer. Had there been a 2013 Brit award for **ubiquity**, she would have bagged it too. On her final night in London, night number nine of this UK tour, a year and a bit on from the release of her highly successful debut album, *Our Version of Events*, Sandé, though, retains all the **vim** of a **debutant**, despite two years of working this same material. Her voice has probably grown stronger with use...

Sandé's ascent has been rapid and thorough: the biggest-selling album of 2012, attendant Brits, Mobos and sundry magazine gongs. This jamminess spread all the way to the crusts at the Olympics, which she sliced both ways, performing in the heroic opening ceremony and the more low-brow mop-up at the end...

Ask any artist: overexposure is a very nice problem to have. Tonight Sandé remains naturally warm and chatty, even when spouting the usual things – 'thanks', 'incredible', 'amazing', 'this song is dedicated to all of you' – that artists spout when the stages they are standing on are bigger than a squash court. Her hair is still a signature shock of blond shaved at the sides, but it has changed in small but significant ways. Where once it was more of a vertical Mohican, now it's a nicely curled 'do': softer, more feminine, less electric.

There are a few more small but telling developments. Sandé's **valedictory** set tonight begins with Heaven, an early single. But its drum'n'bass shuffle has been swapped for a bigger, thwackier, soul-rock sound: her drummer is a man-mountain who makes himself heard all night. Breaking the Law, meanwhile, sounds more and more like U2 as it builds and crests.

Ever since Sandé climbed over the mixing desk (figuratively speaking) around 2011, trading her many backroom songwriting credits for the spotlight, she has presented a visual/auditory **conundrum**: how can a woman with a giant tattoo of Frida Kahlo down her arm sound so tame? Professional disser Noel Gallagher recently dismissed Sandé's music as being 'for grannies', and there's truth in that. Several generations are present tonight, the way they are at Adele gigs.

10 Assessment: Writing a Feature Article

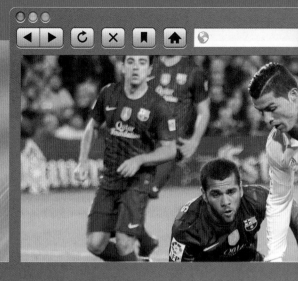

A new website for teenagers is running a series of articles about topics which interest young people. The editor has asked you to write a feature article about something that interests you. For example, it could be about a hobby, such as sport, or a subject like social networking, or an argument for better youth facilities, or an opinion on a famous person.

Use what you've learned in this unit to write an engaging, informative and entertaining feature article.

ome   @ Connect   # Discover

MR MYSTERY

Bookmole
Communist pigs stage
human farmers, but the
become farmers themse

Deanmean

Before you write...

Plan:

- Make sure you have plenty to say about your chosen subject.

- Think about what 'angle' you will take to hook your reader, and a suitable heading.

- Consider your audience carefully and which writing tone is appropriate.

- Decide whether you will include quotations, statistics and facts as well as opinions.

- Think about how you will structure your article, using paragraphs.

As you write...

Review and edit: Check that you are following your plan, keeping your aims in mind, reading and re-reading what you have written to make sure it makes sense and is creating the effect you want to achieve.

When you have finished writing...

Proofread: Check that what you have written is clear and accurate, with correct punctuation and spelling. Check particularly for errors that you know you tend to make in your writing.

5

Young Entrepreneurs

I'm out.

You're fired!

What skills do you need to create a successful business?

ICE CREAM

Introduction

Would you like to set up and run your own business? Thousands of people do, every year. Some are hugely successful; others quickly fail, but most successful entrepreneurs know that the key is to learn from your mistakes, hone your business skills and try again – and again!

This unit explores some of the skills that are essential for a successful business. They include the ability to research information, make careful decisions, present yourself and your ideas in a credible way, and communicate effectively with people both within and outside your business. At the end of the unit you will have the opportunity to create a pitch for possible investors in your new business idea, using the skills you have explored and practised throughout the unit.

ignite INTERVIEW

Renée Watson, Business founder and owner

When you are coming up with a business idea you have got to do something you are really passionate about. No-one is going to be there telling you that you have got to do the job. You have got to motivate yourself to do it. Think about why anyone else is going to be interested in your idea, your product, your service. Think about how you are going to convince them that it is something that is worth them being interested in. Where are you going to be in five years' time? Why are people still going to be interested? How is it going to make money?

✎ Activity

1 Think of a well-known business person (they do not have to be in the photos on this page). List the qualities and skills that you think may have helped them to become successful. Be prepared to explain why.

1 Gap in the Market

↺ Objective

Use inference to select information from non-fiction texts.

All new businesses start with an idea. Business owners try to fill a 'gap in the market' – this is often a product or service that people will buy which isn't already available or, at least, not in a sufficiently appealing way.

✎ Activities

1 In pairs or small groups, list a number of significant products and identify what gap in the market they aimed to fill. You could consider technological products, communication devices, transport and so on.

Richard Branson and Kanya King are both highly successful business people. Read the extracts on page 109, which explain how, as young entrepreneurs, they recognized gaps in the market and decided to launch their new businesses.

📖 Glossary

inference a conclusion about something, based on evidence

2 There may be some unfamiliar words in the extracts, such as 'distribution', 'floundering' and 'turnout'. Try to work out the meanings of these words, using the context of the sentence and thinking about words with a similar root. Check your ideas in a dictionary.

3 What do these extracts tell you about the skills of these young entrepreneurs? You will need to make **inferences** and refer to evidence in the text.

📚 Support

Look for evidence of the following skills in the extracts:

determination   creativity   observation

teamwork

resilience   awareness of market

4 In your own words, summarize the two 'gaps in the market' that these entrepreneurs observed.

In his autobiography, *Losing My Virginity*, Richard Branson describes his idea to set up a mail-order record business linked to the magazine he published and edited, *Student*.

Director magazine describes how Kanya King came to set up the MOBO music awards.

Extract from *Losing My Virginity* by Richard Branson

I thought about the high cost of records and the sort of people who bought *Student* magazine, and wondered whether we could advertise and sell cheap mail-order records through the magazine. As it turned out, the first advertisement for mail-order records appeared in the final edition of *Student*. Without Nik to manage *Student*'s distribution, it was floundering, but the offer of cheap records brought in a flood of inquiries and more cash than we had ever seen before.

We decided to come up with another name for the mail-order business: a name that would be eye-catching, that could stand alone and not just appeal to students... 'Slipped Disc' was one of the favourite suggestions. We toyed with it for a while, until one of the girls leant forward:

'I know,' she said. 'What about "Virgin"? We're complete virgins at business.'

Extract from *Director* magazine article about Kanya King

Today she [Kanya King] has plenty to smile about. At MOBO she employs hundreds of people, staging the largest urban music awards show in Europe, attracting 250 million viewers worldwide. She founded the MOBOs in 1996, having noticed that there was nowhere for artists, who played the music she loved, to showcase their talent. 'I was surrounded by great musicians who weren't getting the recognition they deserved, so as a hobby I was organizing gigs and music events in my spare time, and the turnout was incredible,' she explains.

Later, while working as a television researcher, the opportunity to stage the first MOBO awards came along. She had been knocking on many doors seeking backing for her idea of an award show for music of black origin, but was repeatedly turned away by people who claimed there was no audience.

🕐 Extra Time

Do some research about another successful entrepreneur and find out what gap in the market they decided to fill.

② Choosing the Big Idea

↻ Objective

Make a sustained contribution to group discussion, listening carefully, asking relevant questions, exploring and developing your own ideas and those of other people.

As a team of young entrepreneurs, it's now your turn to try to identify a gap in the market and to develop ideas for a new business.

✏ Activities

1 Most new businesses focus on one of three areas:

- developing a product to sell either through a retail outlet or online (e.g. apps, sports equipment, games, fashion items)

- offering a service of some kind (e.g. cleaning, catering, chauffeuring, recruitment, advice)

- creating a venue for an activity (e.g. a café, sports facility, hotel, visitor attraction).

Choose an area that appeals to you and find others who want to focus on the same area to work with in a group.

Sticky notes that can be repeatedly stuck and removed without damaging what they attach to

Baby cups that don't spill if they are dropped

Treadmills for dogs that cannot be taken out for walks

2 Share your ideas as a group. Make sure that everyone has time to speak, uninterrupted, and others listen carefully, asking questions, making suggestions and building on each other's ideas.

Support

If your ideas dry up, think about a problem or an inconvenience that you have come across. Many of the best new business ideas are developed in response to problems.

3 Use notes to record your ideas. You might want to allocate the role of note-taker to someone in the group. They could record your group's thoughts on a display board as a list, mind map, diagram or grid.

Progress Check

Copy out the grid below. Ask your group to give you a rating between 1–3 (3 being the highest) as to how well you displayed the skills in the grid below.

Skill	Rating
Explained your ideas clearly	
Listened to others' ideas carefully	
Asked relevant questions	
Explored	
Built on other people's ideas	
Kept focused on the topic of discussion	
Performed an allocated role, e.g. note-taker	

After considering the feedback, write down a target for improving one aspect of your speaking and listening skills.

4 Make a shortlist of your three favourite ideas and discuss them in more detail. Consider:

- who would be your target market
- what would be the **USP** for your product or service
- what you would need to set up your business.

5 Take a group vote to decide which one business has the most potential. This is the business idea that you will have to plan a **pitch** for.

ignite INTERVIEW

'First and foremost think about something that excites you. Think about why anyone else is going to be interested in your idea, your product, your service.'

Renée Watson

Glossary

USP unique selling point, something original and different about the product

pitch a speech used to persuade investors to invest in your business idea

3 Planning Your New Business

↻ Objective

Understand and use specialist vocabulary confidently in order to plan and discuss business concepts.

Once you have chosen your business, you need to make plans on how to develop it. Read the interview on page 113, in which Kanya King explains how she developed the MOBO awards and what her future plans are.

✎ Activities

1 A number of words and phrases have been underlined in the interview opposite. Match up the definitions, below, with the underlined words and phrases opposite. Note that the definitions are in a random order.

ignite INTERVIEW

'You need to understand who it is that you are going to be pitching this to, who you are going to be talking to, why they are going to like it. And then think about how you are going to put together a package of information that is going to convince them that this is the best idea that they have ever heard of.'

Renée Watson

someone who puts money into a business scheme in the hope that it will make a profit

an organization that lends money to businesses

take out an extra loan against the value of a property

Internet sites where you can explain an idea or business and people can offer money to be part of it

spread the practice further

part of the ownership

the aims, quality and ethos that are associated with the company

📖 Glossary

perseverance   the quality of being able to continue with an action despite setbacks

gratification   satisfaction

2a How did Kanya King raise finances (money) for her product?

2b How does she promote and market (advertise) her event to others?

↔ **Stretch**

How does she plan for the long-term viability of her business (making sure it has a future)?

Extract from interview by the Female Entrepreneur Association with Kanya King

How did you get started?

I took a risk because I was on a mission to produce a televised event that celebrated a type of music that wasn't being represented in other major events. My overwhelming passion led me to remortgage my home to fund my new company and produce the very first MOBO Awards Show.

What advice would you give to others who are looking to raise finance?

First you need to know how much money you need, what type of lending institution you want to work with, and whether or not you are prepared to give up partial ownership of the company. Look for finance six months before it is needed. There are several sources to consider when looking for financing. Explore all of your options before making a decision. There are many other finance solutions besides family and friends, such as crowd funding platforms where you pitch an idea and potential investors can review the pitches and decide if there are any they would like to fund. They are rewarded if the project comes to fruition.

What are your top pieces of advice for entrepreneurs?

Having self-belief, **perseverance**, clear goals, being able to overcome obstacles and aspiring to greater things. Understanding there is no 'instant **gratification**' when you're running your own business.

What's next for the MOBO Organization?

We'll build on the success of our recent projects by continuing to champion emerging talent and supporting the British Urban music scene as part of the MOBO legacy. We want to build on our successful partnership with HTC with a series of initiatives and showcases throughout the year including our nationwide MOBO Tour offering audiences the opportunity to see some of the freshest, new, emerging talent.

This year we had our inaugural Celebrate MOBO festival in the lead up to the awards which is a series of public events such as industry academy workshops and seminars inspiring young people to get into music, fashion and film. The festival created the opportunity for the local community to join with MOBO in celebrating the achievements of British culture. We are looking to roll out some of these initiatives in conjunction with HTC, who share our deep rooted brand values and our commitment to pushing the boundaries in music. Watch this space!

More to explore

✎ Activities continued

3 Divide your group to plan and discuss two different areas of your business:

- finances and investment
- marketing and promotion.

Each subgroup should discuss and prepare a mini-feedback session to the whole group, outlining what they propose and why.

Use the prompts on page 115 to guide your subgroup discussions.

4 Ask someone from each subgroup to give a mini-presentation on their ideas for finance/investment or marketing/promotion to the whole group. You might find the following tips helpful.

1. Jot down your ideas as prompt notes that you can refer to if necessary, although do not read directly from them.

2. Try to use business terminology in order to clarify your ideas and to practise talking about them.

3. Remember to express your ideas clearly and carefully, speaking slowly. Look at your audience and try not to fidget.

4. Encourage people to ask you questions, to ensure they listen carefully and also to give you practice in explaining your ideas.

€ $ £ ¥

87% 36% 24% 74%

1 2 8 9 10 11 12 13

Finances and investment

- What type of investors are you looking for?

- Do you want people who can offer advice and expertise as well as money?

- Are you prepared to give them partial ownership of your business? If so, what percentage? (Think carefully about how much control you want to retain in the business.)

- How might you find investors? Will you approach people you know or use a crowd funding platform? What might be the advantages and disadvantages of each?

- Is there someone in your family who might be prepared to remortgage a property in order to finance your business?

- If you borrow money from a bank, what are the best interest rates you can find? (Remember that you pay interest in addition to repaying the money that you borrow.)

Marketing and promotion

- What is your target market? (Think about age, gender, background and interests.)

- How is it best to reach your target market? (Think about where they go, how they communicate and where they pick up information.)

- Will you print publicity material, such as posters and leaflets?

- Will you advertise on the TV, radio and online? If so, around what sort of programmes or websites?

- Will you promote your business in public places? If so, where and when?

- What are the key messages and information that you want to convey about your business?

- Is there any competition for your business? If so, what is it? How can you ensure that what you offer is better, cheaper or more desirable?

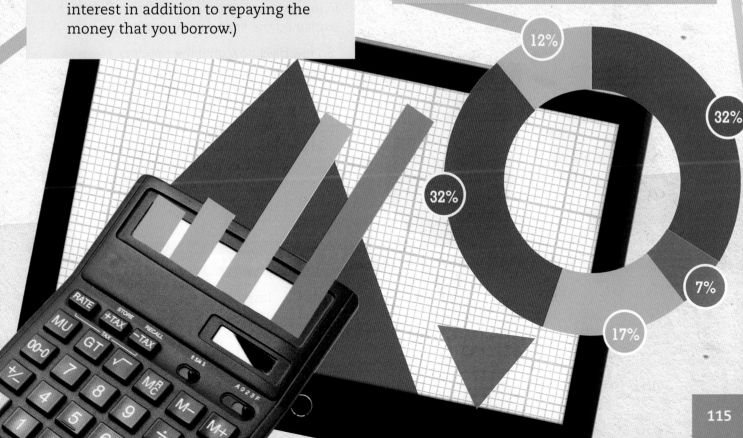

4 Levels of Formality

↻ Objective

Identify and use appropriate levels of formality in writing, depending on audience and context.

When developing your own business, you need to communicate with lots of different people and organizations, often in writing. The level of formality that you use will depend on your relationship with those people.

Read the extract on the right from Richard Branson's autobiography. Note that it includes part of a letter that he wrote to his father while he was at boarding school.

Extract from *Losing My Virginity* by Richard Branson

The following Christmas Nik's brother was given a budgerigar as a present. This gave me the idea for another great business opportunity: breeding budgies! For a start, I reasoned, I could sell them all year round rather than just during the fortnight before Christmas. I worked out the prices and made some calculations about how fast they could breed and how cheap their food was, and persuaded my father to build a huge **aviary**. In my last week at school I wrote to Dad and explained the financial implications:

'So few days now until the holidays. Have you ordered any materials we might want for our giant budgerigar cage? I thought our best bet to get the budgerigars at reduced rate would be from Julian Carlyon. I feel that if the shops sold them for 30**sh.**, he would get say 17sh. and we could buy them off him for 18 or 19sh. which would give him a profit and save us the odd 10sh. per bird. How about it?'

📖 Glossary

aviary   large cage for birds

sh.   shilling, British coin used until February 1971

Bargain Budgies

Going Cheep!

✎ Activities

1 Which words, phrases, abbreviations and sentence structures show that Branson's letter is informal? Explain with close reference to the text. **SPAG**

2 If Richard were writing as an adult to a potential investor that he didn't know, how would his letter be different, both in presentation and language?

▧ Support

Think about the layout of a formal letter, including addresses, date, greeting, paragraphing and an appropriate sign off.

3 Draft a formal letter to a potential investor for your own new business idea. **SPAG**

- Plan how you will divide up your paragraphs, in order to cover all the information that you want to convey. Your plan should include key words that sum up the topic of each paragraph, such as the introduction, description of the new product/service, explanation of market research, and proposed finances.

- Use an appropriate formal greeting and sign off.

- Include clear facts, statistics and dates.

- Use Standard English. Avoid colloquialisms and slang.

- When you have drafted your letter, proofread it for spelling errors and check the punctuation and grammar are correct.

☑ Progress Check

Swap your letter with another student.

Check they have:

- used a suitable greeting and sign off

- divided their paragraphs into clear topics

- used Standard English in a formal, clear, precise way

- used spelling, punctuation and grammar correctly.

Note in pencil any errors or suggestions for improvement before swapping back your letters.

Looking at your own letter again, write down one aspect of formal letter-writing that you will try to improve.

⏱ Extra Time

Branson's business idea was unsuccessful because he had too many budgerigars and not enough customers. Find another example of a successful business person who had an early business failure.

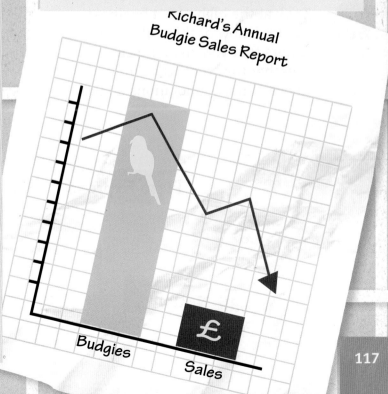

Richard's Annual Budgie Sales Report

Budgies

Sales

£

5 Names and Associations

↻ Objective

Understand how to select vocabulary and craft phrases in order to create a specific reaction in the target reader.

Once you have an idea for a business you must decide on a name for your product or company. Ideally, a product or company name should:

- be memorable
- be fairly simple and easy to spell
- convey some information about your company or product
- have suitable **connotations** for your target market.

✎ Activities

1 Look at the high-street business names below or think of some others that you know. Discuss whether they meet the criteria above. What connotations do they carry?

2 James Caan is a successful entrepreneur. Read the extract on page 119 where he describes how he chose the name for his new business in the 1980s. If he asked you to help him update the image of his company, what alternative names would you suggest? (Think about the connotations that the new name should have. Jot down some key words to get your ideas started.)

3 Think up some possible names for your new company. Use the bullet list on the left to help you and follow some of the strategies described by James Caan. Share and discuss your ideas and then decide on a final name.

Lush

Pizza Express

Games Workshop

Topshop

Next

Poundland

Noodle Nation

Extract from *Start Your Business in 7 Days* by James Caan

And then I named the business to make it mine. I looked at what the other **headhunting** businesses were called. At the time the main companies included Korn/Ferry, Russell Reynolds, Spencer Stuart and Heidrick & Struggles. All these people existed: there was a real Russell Reynolds, for example. I thought, *Ok, there's a tip here. They are normally called after people.* But I didn't like the idea of calling it after me because, to me, that would sound like a one man band. 'Hi, it's James Caan from James Caan Associates.' Somebody taking that call would just know they were being phoned by one guy operating on his own out of a tiny office.

The name, I thought, should say 'Big', 'Established'. As I said those words out loud, I wrote them down in my pad. I added 'Professional', '**Integrity**', 'Dynamic'. I was describing what the business did. I wrote down a whole list of words, and then I thought if that was a person, what would it be called? I looked at my notes and, don't ask me why, but the name Alexander came into my mind. It felt right, because Alexander seemed established, professional.

I carried on **musing**… 'That's quite a long first name, it needs a fairly small surname, otherwise it's too much of a mouthful on the phone.' Very practical thoughts. But I couldn't come up with a surname. I got stuck. I tried a different tack: who is this business going to place in jobs, what kind of people are we going to be dealing with? They are all bankers, economists, senior executives. I wrote down the job titles and they were (and remember this was the 1980s) all men. I wrote down Man, and added an extra 'n'! Alexander Mann. That was a name that suggested substance, integrity, **gravitas**.

⏰ Extra Time

Write a short article for other new entrepreneurs, explaining the importance of getting the name right for their new product.

📖 Glossary

connotations ideas or feelings that a word triggers, in addition to its main, literal meaning

headhunting finding the right person for a job

integrity truthfulness

musing thinking

gravitas seriousness

6 Premises and Finance

↻ Objective

Explore techniques to summarize and present information clearly and concisely.

✎ Activities

1 Decide where you need to locate your business.

- Do you need **retail** or office space? If so, does it need to be in the high street or with a lot of land or parking, or near major transport routes?

- Will it be a mobile business run from a van?

- Will you go to the customer's home?

- Will you be creating events based in different locations?

- Will the business be based online and can you work from home?

📖 Glossary

retail   for selling goods to the general public

2a Write a 'Wanted' advertisement for a local paper or online website, giving details of what you need. (If you don't need premises, focus on equipment.) You will need to pay for each word you use so, to keep your costs down, try to make it as brief, concise and accurate as possible.

2b Swap your advertisement with a partner. Suggest ways of making your partner's advertisement shorter and more precise. Think about the use of vocabulary, cutting out unnecessary words, including key information, using abbreviations and correct punctuation for clarity.   **SPAG**

2c Swap your drafts again and finalize your own advertisement, taking into account your partner's feedback.

When setting up a new business, you need to draw up a financial plan. This will basically list what you expect your **costs** to be and your **income**. The difference between the two will be your **profit** – assuming that your income is higher than your costs. If it isn't, then your business will make a **loss**.

📖 Glossary

costs the money you spend on your business

income the money you earn from your business

profit the extra money you make from your business, after costs have been taken out

loss the amount of money you spend on your business that is not covered by your income

3 Draw up a list of the costs that you think will be involved in your business in the first year. These can be very rough estimates, but try to get an overall figure. Your costs will depend on your type of business. You may want to consider some of these items:

4a Estimate what total income you think you will get from your business. (This is called gross profit and is not your final profit.)

4b Subtract your costs from your gross profit – this will leave your net profit, which is the real money that you have made. This is a very important figure and will interest any potential investors.

4c You will need to summarize this information very clearly and simply when you pitch your business idea to an investor. Experiment with visual ways of showing your financial plan so that it can be displayed, e.g. as a diagram. You could use a pie chart or a graph, for example, to show the differences between your costs, income and profit.

↔ Stretch

Think how you might expand your business beyond the first year. How could you make it grow and increase your profits?

Premises (rent)

Equipment, products or raw materials

Petrol

Web design

Cost of manufacturing

Vehicle

Salaries

Advertising

7 Personality Sells

↻ Objective

Explore the use of verbal and non-verbal techniques to promote and sell a product.

> People buy from people. Remember that you are your brand – and anything is possible.
>
> *Levi Roots, creator of Reggae Reggae Sauce*

> When you're speaking, …you should be firmly rooted into the ground for most of the time. Think of yourself as a tree where the bottom half of your body is the trunk and fixed and the top half is the branches which can move in the breeze.
>
> *From Dragons' Den: The Perfect Pitch*

> What the Dragons taught me is that sometimes what you lack in resources, you can more than make up with the level of your enthusiasm and your energy.
>
> *Imran Hakim, creator of the iTeddy*

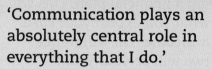

ignite INTERVIEW

'Communication plays an absolutely central role in everything that I do.'

Renée Watson

✎ Activities

1 Read the quotations on the left, which all give advice about promoting a business or product. What do they teach?

2a Look at the song on page 123 that Levi Roots used to introduce his business pitch for **Reggae** Reggae Sauce. Read the annotations by brand manager Shah Khan, which explain the persuasive effect of the words.

2b Using what you learned from the song and the annotations, list some key techniques that you could use in your own persuasive advertising.

3 Write a short pitch of a few lines that you could use in a marketplace to sell your own business idea quickly and briefly to passing people. This could be a song, rhyme or a few persuasive phrases.

↔ Stretch

Develop your ideas into a complete advertisement for TV.

4 Think about how you could add visual impact to your words by what you wear, hold, do or display.

Reggae Reggae Sauce song

Put some music in my food for me → Reminds people of the USP – a flavour from the Caribbean

Gimme some reggae reggae sauce → Tells you Levi likes it

Hot reggae reggae sauce → Tells people what it is

It's so nice I had to name it twice → Explains the name

I called it reggae reggae sauce → Repeats it so people get the message

Hot reggae reggae sauce → Now people really get it!

Just like my baby it's the perfect delight → Makes it sound irresistible

It's got some peppers and some herbs and spice → Explains the ingredients

We want some reggae reggae sauce → Hints at the demand

Hot reggae reggae sauce → Reinforces the message

So nice with your fried chicken, makes burgers finger-licking, on rice and peas and fish → Tells you what to do with it

Put some reggae reggae sauce on your lips. → Reinforces the whole message

☑ Progress Check

Present your short persuasive pitch to another student.

Ask them to comment on whether you use:

- an appropriate **tone of voice**
- appropriate body language, gestures and facial expressions
- persuasive devices in what you say, e.g. memorable names or statements, repetition, key words, questions, attractive images
- confidence and enthusiasm
- appropriate informal or formal language, depending on the product.

After listening to the feedback, write a target for your next persuasive pitch.

📖 Glossary

reggae type of music originating from Jamaica

tone of voice the way words are spoken, e.g. a serious tone, a light-hearted tone, etc.

8 Responding to Questions

↻ Objective

Develop techniques for effective listening, questioning and responding to others during role-play.

Most successful entrepreneurs will be skilled not only in answering questions asked by investors and colleagues, but also at asking pertinent questions, for example when interviewing potential staff.

Read the advice about responding to questions from an audience in the extract opposite from *Dragons' Den: The Perfect Pitch* by Peter Spalton.

✎ Activities

1 Which techniques recommended in the extract could also be applied to responding to questions during a job interview?

2a Role-play an interview with another student, who wants to work in your business. Think of a possible job vacancy in your business and list some of the skills you would need in your employee.

2b Write some questions to find out whether the potential employee has these skills and would be suited to your company. Avoid questions that could be answered with 'yes' or 'no'.

◈ Support

Example questions:

- Describe a situation where you have shown success. What led to your success? (This checks their strengths.)

- What is your biggest weakness? (This checks honesty and willingness to improve.)

2c Complete the interviews in small groups with one potential employee and two or three others on the interview panel, asking questions. Take it in turns to be the potential employee.

2d Give feedback to each person interviewed.

- Make sure you say something positive and aim to help them improve.

- Would you give them a job? Give one or two reasons for your answer.

Extract from *Dragons' Den: The Perfect Pitch* by Peter Spalton

Follow these seven simple steps, whatever the question is.

1   Turn towards the person asking the question and look at them. Concentrate on them and nod occasionally to show them that you're listening.

2   Demonstrate that you take their questions seriously by **suppressing** your own emotions...

3   Listen intently and don't interrupt. Imagine they're giving you a piece of vital information such as the phone number of someone you're desperate to contact. Notice the tone of their voice. Is it genuine, insecure or **hostile**? Try and work out what the point of their question is and what they really want to know.

4   Clarify the question if it sounds **obtuse** or complex. Sometimes people jumble up two or three points in a single question. If they do, say something like, 'Let me just check, you're asking if…?'.

5   Pause for a second then answer the question clearly and distinctly in a serious sounding voice. Show empathy and respect by saying something like, 'I know it can be a bit confusing' or 'That's a good point, let me…'. Do not attack the person who asked the question or put them in their place. Audiences have much more in common with each other than they do with you. If you **alienate** one, they will all gang up against you.

6   **Address** the rest of the room when you answer the question.

7   When you've finished, stop and smile at the person who asked the question. Slightly tilt your head as though you're asking them if it's okay. They may say 'Thank you.' If they don't you must check that they are happy with the answer you've given. You should say something like, 'Does that answer your question?'

📖 Glossary

suppressing   hiding or controlling

hostile   unfriendly; aggressive

obtuse   difficult to understand

alienate   anger; distance

address   speak to

🕐 Extra Time

Watch a clip from *Dragons' Den*. Write a short paragraph about the entrepreneur's skill in listening and responding to questions. Focus on their strengths and their weaknesses.

9 Preparing the Pitch

↻ Objectives

- Analyse a successful pitch, noting techniques that are effective and can be used for other pitches.

- Prepare a pitch, using effective planning, drafting and rehearsing techniques.

When you present a pitch to potential business investors you need to give a clear description of your concept, present a credible financial plan and convince them that you are passionate and committed to developing your new business. You need to plan your pitch carefully, write it out in full, then rehearse it, finalize it and make notes that you can glance at during the presentation.

Before you start preparing your own pitch, read the extract on page 127. It records a successful pitch to investors by Sammy French for her canine treadmill, which she developed after finding it difficult to keep her dogs fit when she was recovering from an operation. Sammy's business is called Fit Fur Life. She began her pitch by demonstrating the treadmill with her dog, Daffy.

✎ Activities

1 How does Sammy prove that her product works?

2 What does Sammy say to convince the Dragons that her product will make money?

3 Look again at the extract from Sammy's pitch. Identify in the pitch where Sammy:

    A describes the target market and potential customers

    B explains what the money will be used for

    C explains the investment needed and percentage of the company offered

    D demonstrates the product.

4 Do you think the name for Sammy's business is a good one? Why?

Extract from *Dragons' Den: Success, From Pitch to Profit*

Sammy asked for £100,000 for 25 per cent of her business. She pointed out that there was a large market for her treadmill: over 200,000 people train dogs in the professional industry such as vets and the police force; kennels and rescue centres would find her treadmill invaluable; and in the UK there are a further 5 million people who either own or work with dogs. She demonstrated the finely adjustable incline and decline features of the treadmill, and told the Dragons:

'I've tested this market with a previous model and I've sold 147 units. I am having to turn away business, because I simply cannot supply the demand for this product at this stage. What I would like to do with any investment is to finance the **production run** of the first 150 machines and then the sales generated from that will fully **capitalise** all the working requirements of the company and any future **stock**.'

📖 Glossary

production run   making of the product in a factory

capitalise   supply with money; fund

stock   product that is ready to be sold

30%?!

I'm out.

ignite INTERVIEW

'What you want to do is enthuse people with the excitement that you have for your idea and then give them all the back up to convince them that actually it has got substance.'

Renée Watson

More to explore

127

✎ Activities continued

5 Now it's your turn. Follow the steps below to prepare the pitch for your business.

1 Planning

First, gather your ideas together. They don't have to be in any particular order at this stage and you can record them in a way that is most effective for you, e.g. as a list, a mind map or on sticky notes on a board.

Think about:

- what the product or service is
- how much the product or service would cost
- who would be likely to buy the product or service (target market or customer)
- a visual illustration or image for the product, or a demonstration
- the location of the product or service, or how it will be delivered
- the amount of investment needed and the percentage of the business you would offer in return
- what you would spend the investment on and why
- persuasive devices and techniques
- anything else that would persuade the investors.

Then order your ideas into groups and decide on a logical sequence that will form the basic structure of your pitch.

2 Drafting

Write out your pitch. Keep re-reading it and making improvements. If you can't decide on suitable wording, leave a gap and revisit it. Keep reciting it aloud, making sure it feels logical and fluent.

Note in your written pitch where you will demonstrate or display something, so that you know what order to do things in.

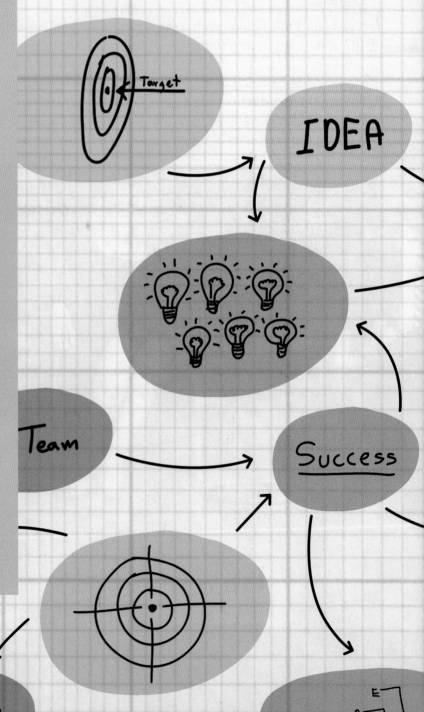

3 Rehearsing

When you are happy with your pitch, do a full rehearsal of it in front of a partner. Give each other constructive feedback, commenting on areas that were done well and areas that need improvement. Make sure that you give each other feedback and continue to practise, change and improve your pitches.

Check that you:

- show confidence and enthusiasm when you speak

- explain your product clearly

- emphasize your product's USP

- show that the investor's money will be spent wisely

- use visuals or demonstrations effectively

- remember what you learned earlier in the unit about the way that you stand, your gestures and expressions

- speak clearly and not too fast. Decide which words you want to emphasize and where to pause for effect. Use the tone and volume of your voice carefully.

4 Preparing notes

Taking on board your partner's comments, revise your pitch, making it as concise and effective as possible. Make short note cards that you can use during your pitch to remind you of what you want to say. You should not read out your pitch, but look directly at your audience as you speak, only glancing down occasionally at your notes.

🕒 Extra Time

Watch a successful pitch from a show such as *The Apprentice*. Note what you think made it successful and try to incorporate some of these aspects into your own pitch.

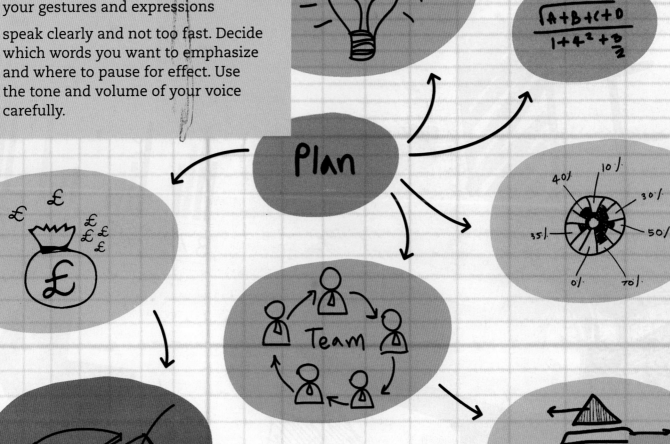

$$\frac{\sqrt{A+B+C+D}}{1+4^2+\frac{B}{2}}$$

Plan

Team

10 Assessment: Making Your Pitch

Two successful business partners have decided to help set up a new business. They have asked for ideas to be presented to them. They will choose the most compelling proposition. Your task is to present your pitch to them with the aim of winning their financial backing and expertise.

You will need to:

- deliver your pitch with confidence and enthusiasm
- back up what you say with a demonstration or visuals
- answer questions from the investors.

Note that you are being tested on your spoken English skills, rather than your writing skills in this assessment.

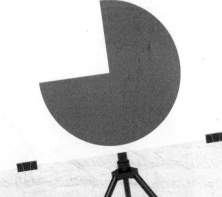

Before you present...

Most people feel nervous in unfamiliar situations. Here are some tips to combat your nerves.

- Make sure you are well prepared and rehearsed. Practise using your prompt cards, but remember not to rely just on them. You should have memorized most of your pitch.

- Picture yourself succeeding. Imagine smiles on your audience's faces and you standing confidently and enthusiastically.

- Focus on the positives. Think about all of the things you have learned rather than anything you are not sure about.

- Absorb yourself in other people's presentations as you wait your turn. Remember that you are all in the same situation.

During and after the presentation...

- If something goes wrong or you are not sure about something, you can ask to start again or say you will find out the information later. Be honest about the situation rather than try to cover something up. If you are honest, the audience will be on your side.

- Make sure you listen to the questions put to you after the pitch. Concentrate fully on what you are asked and aim to give a helpful answer in your response. Remember that you want to keep your audience, the investors, on your side.

From Talking Drums to Tweets

As communications technology advances, how does this change the language we use and the ways that we use it?

Introduction

From talking drums and telegrams to text messages and Twitter, the technology we use to communicate has changed hugely over time. Advances in communications technology have altered the ways we live our lives, changing our behaviour and even the language we use.

In this unit, you will explore the different ways in which communications technology has influenced language, from inventing new vocabulary to changing the ways in which we read, write and speak.

ignite INTERVIEW
Fiona McPherson, Oxford English Dictionary Editor

The *Oxford English Dictionary* is a massive dictionary where we include all meanings of a word. A new meaning of a word will enter the *OED* when we have found enough evidence of its use. The most interesting thing I think about language change is that we tend to look at it just at the point at which we are talking about. But really language change takes an awfully long time to happen. I think everybody is actually fascinated by language even if they don't really realize it. And I think the reason is that it is what we use. It is the tools of communication.

✎ Activities

1 Think about the different ways you have used technology in the last week to:

- communicate with other people
- read for information or for pleasure.

2 Discuss the ways in which technology has changed the way you communicate with friends, family and others.

1 Communication Breakdown

↻ Objective

Analyse and respond to different viewpoints and present your own views on an issue.

We often think of technological change as a positive phenomenon, but how might the technology we use to communicate have a negative effect on the way we live? Read the newspaper article on page 135 and then complete the activities below.

✎ Activities

1 Identify the negative effects of communications technology listed in the article.

2 Discuss the ways in which communications technology has improved people's manners, e.g. being able to text somebody to let them know you are going to be late.

3 Do you think that mobile phones, laptops and social media have made people ruder? Give examples to support your point of view.

4 Discuss and agree a set of rules to help people avoid being rude in the way they use modern technology, e.g. *Don't look at your mobile phone when somebody is talking to you.*

▧ Support

Remember to use **imperative** verbs when writing your rules. **SPAG**

5 Design a poster or flier to appear in your school that either promotes the benefits of using communications technology or encourages people to use communications technology in a considerate manner.

HOW MOBILES HAVE CREATED A GENERATION WITHOUT MANNERS:
THREE IN FOUR PEOPLE THINK PHONES, LAPTOPS AND SOCIAL MEDIA HAVE MADE US RUDER

For anyone who has had to wait for service while a shop assistant finished surfing the net on a smartphone, it will not come as a shock.

The latest handsets and other mobile devices may be helping a new generation to stay safer and better connected... but it's making them ruder.

About three in four people now believe manners have been wrecked by phones, laptops, tablets and social media such as Facebook and Twitter, according to a poll by the modern **etiquette** guide Debrett's.

Some 77 per cent think social skills are worse than 20 years ago, while 72 per cent think mobiles have encouraged rudeness. A report warned that company executives are now watching to check if their young employees are becoming over-dependent on their smartphones and screens in the office.

Some are 'so over-reliant on computers and spellchecks that they don't even know how to write a letter any more,' one told Debrett's...

The etiquette consultancy also conducted a study among a group of 58 senior executives which found that well over half looked for social skills rather than academic achievement in candidates for promotion.

They believed that a major problem among young employees was 'constant use of mobile phones and social media in the office.' A majority felt the written skills of young employees were 'appalling'.

The report cited 'a **rift** between virtual and real world personalities', saying that 15 per cent of the people in its poll would feel confident walking into a room where they didn't know anybody, while 62 per cent would be confident about creating a profile on a social networking site.

Please switch off your phone

QUIET ZONE
Please refrain from using electronic devices

📖 Glossary

imperative form of verb that is like a command, usually found at the start of a sentence, e.g. *Look..., Make..., Go...*

etiquette rules of correct behaviour

rift divide

2 Smart Phones?

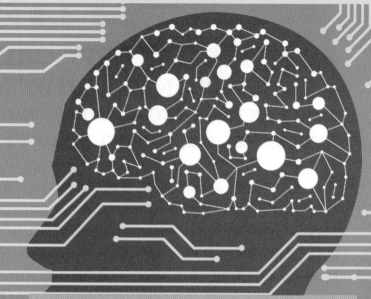

↻ Objective

Consider and discuss views about the positive and negative effects of technological change.

Do you think using modern technology such as laptops and mobile phones can help to make you a more intelligent person? Read the article below about the results of a survey looking at the effects modern technology might have on the brains of young people.

📖 Glossary

gratification   satisfaction

What is today's wired-up world doing to young people's brains? That's what a survey run by the Pew Research Centre in the USA attempted to find out. They interviewed over 1,000 technology experts, critics and students to discover their views on the effects that technology has on young people.

The results of the survey made for interesting reading, with some interesting differences of opinion on show. 55% of the people surveyed agreed with the statement that by the year 2020, the brains of young people would work differently from older people because of their exposure to technology. The positive benefits of these changes in young people's brains included the ability to find answers to questions more quickly. However, 42% of people surveyed shared more pessimistic views about how technology is affecting young people's brains with lack of concentration and a thirst for instant **gratification** being two of the changes identified.

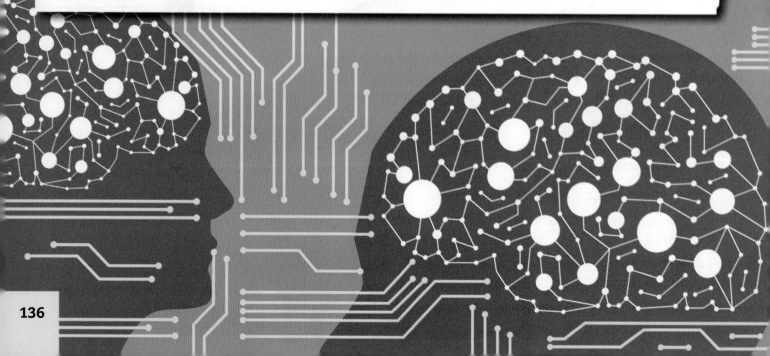

✎ Activities

1 Which of the following statements do you agree with?

> Young people are able to multi-task more effectively than older people and use technology to help them to learn more and develop new skills.

> Young people are easily distracted and find it difficult to think deeply compared to older people, and rely on technology to help them to function.

Think of examples from your own life to support the statement you agree with.

2 Discuss whether you think technology makes people more or less intelligent.

⬢ Support

Consider the different ways technology could help to improve people's knowledge and intelligence, e.g. searching for information online.

3a Look at the list of skills on the right that the **CBI** says young people need in the workplace. Think about the careers you are interested in and rank these skills in order of importance. Give reasons for your choices.

3b Discuss the ways technology could help young people improve each of these skills. What negative effects could technology have on any of these skills?

Workplace skills

- Self-management – readiness to accept responsibility; flexibility; time management; readiness to improve own performance
- Teamworking – respecting others; co-operating; negotiating; persuading; contributing to discussions
- Problem solving – analysing facts and situations and applying creative thinking to develop appropriate solutions
- Communication – ability to produce clear, structured written work; spoken English skills, including listening and questioning
- Numeracy – general mathematical awareness; ability to work with numbers and apply this in practical contexts

4 How do you think technology will change the way we work in the future? What new skills do you think will be needed by employers in the year 2020? Write an email to the CBI explaining your ideas.

📖 Glossary

CBI Confederation of British Industry – an organization representing businesses in the UK

🕐 Extra Time

Interview your friends and family to find out whether they think technological change is making people more or less intelligent.

(3) # Talking Drums

↻ ## Objective

Consider and discuss views about the positive and negative effects of technological change.

MAKE YOUR FEET COME BACK THE WAY THEY WENT

MAKE YOUR LEGS COME BACK THE WAY THEY WENT

Communications technology doesn't just mean the latest model of mobile phone. From the sound of drums to Skype, for hundreds of years every new form of communications technology has influenced the ways in which language is used. Read the extract below, which is taken from James Gleick's book *The Information*. This extract describes how sub-Saharan Africans used 'talking drums' to send messages quickly over long distances.

Extract from *The Information* by James Gleick

No one spoke simply on the drums. Drummers would not say, 'Come back home,' but rather,

Make your feet come back the way they went,

make your legs come back the way they went,

plant your feet and your legs below,

in the village which belongs to us.

They could not just say 'corpse' but would elaborate: 'which lies on its back on clods of earth.' Instead of 'don't be afraid,' they would say, 'Bring your heart back down out of your mouth, your heart out of your mouth, get it back down from there.' The drums generated fountains of **oratory**. This seemed inefficient. Was it **grandiloquence** or **bombast**? Or something else?

The African people who used talking drums spoke in tonal languages where **pitch** alters the meaning of a word. Words that use the same **syllables** mean different things according to the tone in which they are spoken, for example, the word 'liala' means fiancée when the middle 'a' is said with a high-pitched tone, but means 'rubbish pit' when said with three low syllables. The talking drums use only high and low pitched notes to communicate, missing out the consonants and vowels completely. This meant that the drummers had to add little phrases to each short word to make its meaning clear.

📖 ## Glossary

oratory public speaking

grandiloquence long-winded and overblown style of speaking

bombast high-sounding language with little meaning

pitch how high or low your voice is

syllable a word or part of a word that has one vowel sound when you say it, e.g. 'cat' has one syllable, 'din-o-saur' has three syllables.

abstract noun a noun that refers to a concept, such as 'hope', 'trust', 'pride' or 'determination'

✎ Activities

1   Discuss the advantages of using talking drums as a form of communication. What might be the disadvantages?

2   Create your own talking drum phrases for the following words. The first one has been done for you.

Word	Talking drum phrase
Moon	The moon looks down at the earth.
School	
Run	
Spicy	
Slowly	

↔ Stretch

Create talking drum phrases for the following **abstract nouns**:

- bravery
- curiosity
- peace
- trust
- trouble.

3a   Read the sentence below and work out what it means.

If u cn rd ths u cn gt a gd jb w hi pa.

3b   Discuss how this sentence is similar to the language of the talking drums.

☑ Progress Check

Using the same style of sentences as in Activity 2, create a set of instructions for a simple task such as making a cup of tea. Give the instructions to a partner and see if they are able to follow them. Discuss any difficulties they found with the instructions and ways you could communicate this information more clearly.

4 Twitter and Telegrams

↻ Objectives

- Explore how different forms of communications technology influence the way language is used.

- Adapt phrases, sentence structures and conventions to communicate the same information in different media.

New advances in communications technology can sometimes influence language in similar ways to older forms of communication. Read the blog post on page 141 which compares two forms of communications technology: the 21st century social network Twitter; and the telegram which was invented in the 19th century.

✎ Activities

1 Pick out the similarities the writer identifies between Twitter and the telegram.

2 From the blog post, list the techniques used by writers of telegrams and tweets to communicate information concisely. Use these to create a list of tips for users of Twitter to write shorter tweets.

3a Change the following paragraph into a tweet of 140 characters or fewer.

> Good writers are able to express their ideas with simplicity and clarity. They know to avoid including unnecessary details as these often distract the reader and make them less likely to read on. Often the most complex of ideas can be communicated in the simplest of ways.

▧ Support

Use your editing skills to cut any words and phrases that aren't essential. Try to find shorter synonyms for any longer words included in the paragraph.

3b Discuss the changes you have made to transform this paragraph into a tweet. Comment on:

SPAG

- your use of contractions and abbreviations

- any changes you made to the vocabulary and punctuation.

4 Discuss the changes you make to the language you use in the following forms of communication:

- text messages

- emails

- blogs.

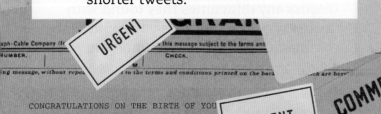

Brevity in communication: Twitter vs the telegram

While Twitter has become a wildly popular new means of communication, it has not been without its critics. Questions like, 'What can we say that is meaningful in 140 characters?' and 'What are we losing by keeping our social interactions so brief?' have abounded since Twitter's inception. The value of **brevity**, however, is not a new concept. In the late 19th and early 20th century, one of the most efficient ways to transmit important information rapidly over great distances was the telegram.

Telegram authors had an incentive to be brief – most telegram companies charged per word. As a result, authors took some common shortcuts used in the **Twitterverse** such as dropping pronouns and articles and using abbreviations and code words to maximize information and minimize characters. So forced brevity in communications isn't really a new concept at all. In fact, telegrams were often used to convey life-changing news – births, deaths, war, and peace – in as few words as possible. Imagine finding out that a loved one has died in a Tweet, or worse, receiving a telegram of **import redacted** to the point of ambiguity. From that perspective, the criticisms of Twitter seem unnecessary, or at least, unoriginal.

Wednesday 10.34   75%

⬇ Pull down to refresh

alexGbell1847   2s
Mr. Watson. come here, I want to see you
#classicquotes

sammyJ1709   4m
@alexGbell1847 yeah mate - like 40,000 #srsly

alexGbell1847   23m
@sammyJ1907 found any new words lately?

🔁 Retweeted

alexGbell1847   47m
The day will come when the man at the telephone
will be able to see the distant person to whom he
is speaking

sammyJ1709   52m
Only nine years in the making but it's now
complete. A Dictionary of the English Language will
be in all good book stores from 15 April 1755

sammyJ1709   4h
Lexicographer: writer of dictionaries; harmless
drudge that busies himself in tracing the original
and detailing the signification of words

alexGbell1847   2d
It's great being on twitter. But it's nothing
compared to my telephone. #itsgoodtotalk

📖 Glossary

brevity   brief or concise

Twitterverse   the social networking site Twitter

import   matters of importance

redacted   edited

ignite INTERVIEW

'In the summer of 2013, the word 'tweet', meaning a posting made on the social networking site, Twitter, was added to the dictionary.'

Fiona McPherson

5 The Printed Word

↻ Objective

Consider the role of the printing press in the development of the English language.

Nowadays, millions of books are printed in English every year, but before the invention of the printing press, every single text had to be written by hand. During the Middle Ages, **illuminated manuscripts** containing beautiful decorations and illustrations were produced by monks in monasteries and later on by professional illuminators based in towns and cities. But in 1476, a man named William Caxton introduced the printing press to England, allowing books to be produced more quickly and cheaply than before.

Look at the extract on the right taken from Geoffrey Chaucer's *The Canterbury Tales*, which was originally written in the 14th century but first printed by Caxton in 1476.

Extract from *The Canterbury Tales* by Geoffrey Chaucer

In tholde dayes of the king Arthour,

Of which that Britons speken greet honour,

Al was this land fulfild of fayerye.

The elf-queen, with hir Ioly companye,

Daunced ful ofte in many a grene mede;

This was the olde opinion, as I rede.

I speke of manye hundred yeres ago;

But now can no man see none elves mo.

📖 Glossary

illuminated manuscript   a manuscript that includes small illustrations, borders and decorated initials

dialect   informal words used in a specific geographical area

The Canterbury Tales was written in Middle English, which a modern-day reader might not be able to instantly understand.

In Caxton's time, several different regional **dialects** of English were spoken across the country. In the books he printed, Caxton used a version of English based on the dialects of London and the south east.

✎ Activities

1 Working in pairs, read the text out loud and think about how each word is pronounced to help you work out its meaning. Don't worry if you can't translate every word, but try to work out the overall meaning of the text.

📚 Support

Try the following strategies to help you work out the meanings of Middle English words.

- Use phonics to break the word down into separate sounds to hear the word, e.g. 'speke' could mean 'speak'.

- Look for groups of letters that are familiar to try to work out the word, e.g. 'tholde dayes' could mean 'the old days'.

2 Write a paragraph explaining what you think the extract says.

3 Share your ideas with another pair. Discuss the differences you have noticed between Middle English and Modern English.

4 Discuss how the introduction of the printing press might have affected the development of a standard form of English.

🕐 Extra Time

What are the modern equivalents of the printing press? Write a short article for your school newspaper that discusses how the creation of books has changed over time.

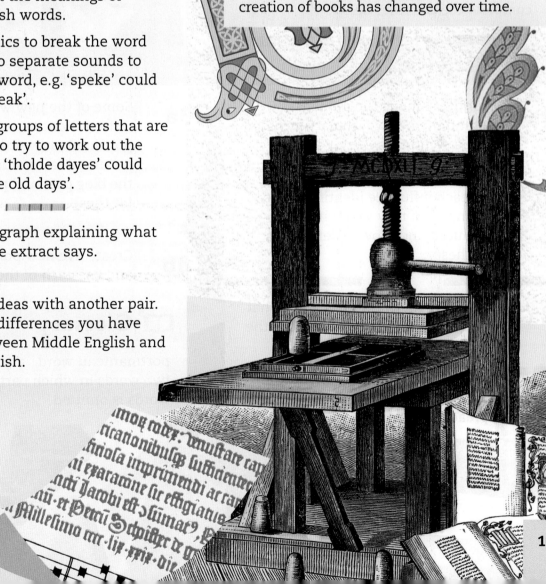

6 From A to Squee!

↻ Objectives

- Investigate the role of the dictionary in the development of the English language.

- Explore how vocabulary develops and changes over time.

New words in the English language are being created all the time. Read the blog post from Oxford Dictionaries Online on page 145 about the new words they have added to their online dictionary and complete the activities below.

✎ Activities

1a Identify some of the influences behind the new vocabulary included in the dictionary.

1b For each influence identified, give examples of new words it has produced and provide definitions for these.

2a Look again at the word 'selfie'. What does the blog post suggest drove the spread of this word?

2b In what other ways could new words spread? Discuss your ideas.

3a Some of the new words added to Oxford Dictionaries Online are **portmanteau words**. Identify the portmanteau words mentioned in the blog post and provide definitions for these.

3b Create five new portmanteau words and use each of these in a sentence.

📖 Glossary

portmanteau word   a combination of two words in which part of one or both words is omitted

Extract from Oxford Dictionaries Online

We've just added some 'srsly buzzworthy' words to our online dictionary – 'squee'! With influences ranging from technology to fashion, there is something for everyone in the update.

If you are someone who always leaves 'prepping' for a party to the last minute, you'll be relieved to know that you can now 'click and collect', so you can avoid a mad 'trolley dash' to grab some 'cake pops' or 'blondies' before your guests arrive. And don't forget some 'pear cider' to wash down all those tasty treats.

Even if your party turns into an 'omnishambles', full of people in 'double denim' doing 'dad dancing', try not to worry. You'll soon feel better after a bit of 'me time': a few minutes in the 'child's pose', a chilled 'michelada', and a 'Nordic noir' will have you feeling as right as rain.

The additions may have only just entered the dictionary, but we've been watching them for a while now, tracking how and where they are used. Two of the words to make their debut in the dictionary, 'selfie' and 'phablet' both featured on our 'Words on the radar' post back in June 2012. At the time, *selfie* featured primarily in social media contexts, but had attracted media attention after Hillary Clinton apparently used the word in a text message to the owner of a Tumblr dedicated to an image of her texting.

'Omnishambles', which is new this quarter, was 'Oxford Dictionaries Word of the Year in 2012'. At the time of choosing, it wasn't clear whether or not it would find its way into one of our dictionaries. But it has continued to gain momentum since then, and is now deserving of an entry.

Several fashion terms also make their Oxford dictionary debut this season including 'flatform', 'geek chic', and 'jorts'. *Jorts* is a good example of a 'blend' (also known as a 'portmanteau'), a word which is a combination of two words in which part of one or both words is omitted (with *jorts* being a blend of jeans and shorts). And it's in good company, with 'babymoon' and 'fauxhawk' also entering the dictionary.

More to explore

The very first English dictionary was published in 1604. This was a slim book with the title *A Table Alphabeticall* and contained approximately 3000 words. Read the extract from this below and then complete the activities.

ignite INTERVIEW

'New words and new meanings of a word will enter the dictionary when we have found enough evidence of their use.'

Fiona McPherson

Extract from *A Table Alphabeticall*

centre, (g) middest of any round thing or circle

centurion, captaine of a hundred men

ceruse, white leade, or painting that women vse

cessement, tribute

chanell, sinke

chaos, (g) a confused heap or mingl-mangle

[fr] **chapelet**, a garland

✎ Activities continued

4 Discuss how helpful you think the definitions provided are. Are there any words you weren't familiar with or didn't understand the meanings of?

5 The writer of the dictionary identifies words that have come from other languages, using (g) and [fr] to indicate words of Greek or French origin. Why do you think he has done this?

↔ Stretch

Instead of organizing this first dictionary alphabetically, the writer could have organized words by meaning into categories, e.g. animals, plants, tools, etc. List the advantages and disadvantages of this approach.

In the earliest printed books, the same word could be found spelt in several different ways even in the same book. Dictionaries helped to fix the spelling of words.

6a Identify any words where the modern-day spelling has changed.

SPAG

6b How important do you think it is to spell correctly?

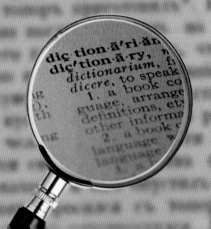

Now read the extract from Samuel Johnson's *A Dictionary of the English Language*, which was published in 1755. Here, he gives his definition for the word 'chaos'.

7 Compare Johnson's definition of the word 'chaos' with the definition from *A Table Alphabeticall*. Which do you find most helpful? You should comment on the information provided and how this is presented.

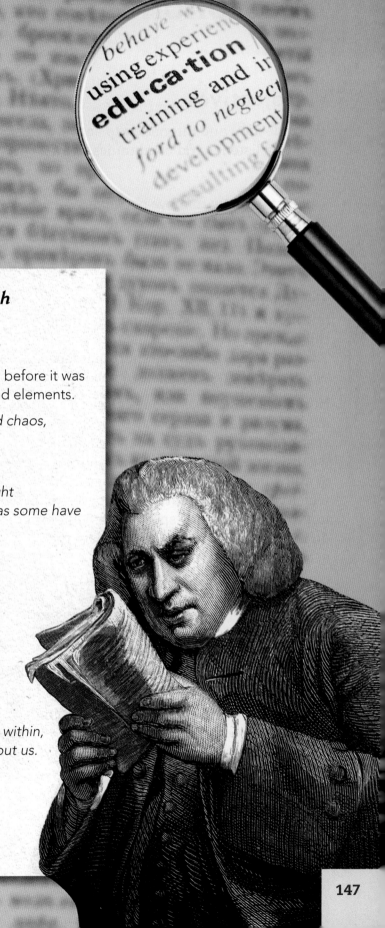

Extract from *A Dictionary of the English Language* by Samuel Johnson

Cháos. n.s. [chaos, Lat.]

1. The mass of matter supposed to be in confusion before it was divided by the creation into its proper classes and elements.

   The whole universe would have been a confused chaos, without beauty or order. – Bentley.

2. Confusion; irregular mixture.

   Had I followed the worst, I could not have brought church and state to such a chaos of confusions, as some have done.
   – K. Charles.

   Their reason sleeps, but mimick fancy wakes,

   Supplies her parts, and wild ideas takes

   From words and things, ill sorted, and misjoin'd,

   The anarchy of thought, and chaos of the mind.

   – Dryden.

3. Any thing where the parts are undistinguished.

   We shall have nothing but darkness and a chaos within, whatever order and light there be in things without us.
   – Locke.

   Pleas'd with a work, where nothing's just or fit,

   One glaring chaos and wild heap of wit.

   – Pope.

7 Telephone Tone

↻ Objectives

- Use inflection and intonation to actively involve a listener and communicate meaning.

- Understand how to move between formal and informal registers in different contexts.

Alexander Graham Bell invented the telephone in 1876 and the first telephone call he made was to his assistant, Thomas Watson, with the short message: 'Mr Watson, come here, I need you.'

Nowadays, billions of phone calls are made every day, but the way that we speak on the telephone and the language we use depends on who we are talking to and why. Read the guide on page 149, which has been written for employees to improve the way they speak to customers on the telephone, and then complete the activities.

✎ Activities

1 How important do you think tone of voice is for telephone communication? Think about the tone of voice you use when speaking on the telephone in different situations.

2 Role-play a phone call to complain about your mobile phone service. Take it in turns to play the part of the customer and the mobile phone employee. Use the following techniques to improve your inflection.

- Smile when you are speaking – this helps your voice to sound warm and friendly.

- Change the stress on certain words to change the meaning of what you say.

◈ Support

Practise asking the question 'What would you like us to do about it?' in different ways:

- emphasizing the words 'would you'

- emphasizing the words 'like us'

- not emphasizing any of the words.

Discuss how the meaning of the question changes when you stress certain words.

Register is the form of language appropriate for different situations, e.g. formal or informal. You might use an informal register when speaking with your friends, but switch to a formal register using Standard English when talking to your Head Teacher.

3 In what situations might you use a formal register when speaking on the phone?

Extract from 'Improving Your Inflection on the Phone'

When you deal with customers over the phone, you have a whole new set of etiquette rules. The minute you pick up the phone, body language disappears, and your **tone of voice** and the words you use become the entire story.

In fact, almost the entire message you project to a customer over the phone is communicated through your tone of voice. For example:

- A **monotone** and flat voice says to the customer, 'I'm bored and have absolutely no interest in what you're talking about.'

- Slow speed and low pitch communicate the message, 'I'm depressed and want to be left alone.'

- A high-pitched and **emphatic** voice says, 'I'm enthusiastic about this subject.'

- An abrupt speed and loud tone say, 'I'm angry and not open to input!'

- High pitch combined with drawn-out speed conveys, 'I don't believe what I'm hearing.'

Inflection is the wave-like movement of highs and lows in the pitch of your voice. The peaks and valleys in your voice let your customers know how interested (or uninterested) you are in what they're saying. Inflection also reflects how interested you are in what you're saying to the customer. When inflection is missing, your voice can sound monotone (read boring and tedious).

📖 Glossary

tone of voice   the way words are spoken, e.g. a serious tone, a light-hearted tone, etc.

monotone   expressionless tone of voice

emphatic   expressed clearly and with power

🕐 Extra Time

Write your own guide to mobile phone etiquette.

'Mr Watson, come here, I need you.'

8 Live News

↺ Objective

Compare the language and structure of live blogging with newspaper reports.

Morning newspapers print yesterday's news today, but in today's world people expect to read up-to-the-minute information. As newspapers have moved online, live blogging has become a format for reporting breaking news stories. Read the extract from the live blog on page 151, reporting on the birth of the Duke and Duchess of Cambridge's baby, and then read the newspaper report on the same event.

✎ Activities

1 Discuss the different ways the live blog and newspaper report present this news story. You should comment on:

- the structure of each text
- the style and formality of the language used
- the way they refer to and include information from other sources.

Support

Newspaper reports begin with the most important information: the 'who', 'what', 'where', 'when', 'why' and 'how' of the story being reported. Think about where the different pieces of this information might appear in a live blog.

2 What are the benefits of reading a live blog over a traditional newspaper report? What are the disadvantages?

↔ Stretch

Explain which format you think is more likely to be accurate in its reporting of the news.

3 Create your own live blog. This could be for a sporting event such as a football match or a breaking news story.

Report
Reporters: Peter Hunt

6.10pm BST A bit of movement now over at the Palace. Peter Hunt, Royal correspondent for the BBC, tweets:

 A helicopter has landed in the grounds of Buckingham Palace. It's not known who was on board. #RoyalBaby

– Peter Hunt (@BBCPeterHunt) July 22, 2013

Well, we can safely rule out one particular royal pilot being at the controls.

7.59pm BST A snippet now from 'Charleswatch' and the Press Association reports that the Prince of Wales was asked if there was any news as he left Harewood House, near Leeds, tonight.

His reply:

No. You'll hear before I do, I suspect.

Perish the thought.

8.30pm BST It's a boy

It's a boy! Eight pounds and six ounces, born at 4.24pm.

8.32pm BST Apparently the boy and his mother are doing well. Kate will be spending the night in hospital. Both families have been informed.

So, the UK is going to have male monarchs for some time to come.

DUCHESS OF CAMBRIDGE GIVES BIRTH TO BABY BOY, THIRD IN LINE TO THE THRONE

Royal couple's first child weighed 8lbs 6oz, Kensington Palace announces

The Duchess of Cambridge gave birth to a son on Monday, the third in line to the throne, a baby destined to be the 43rd monarch since William the Conqueror obtained the English crown in 1066.

Kensington Palace announced at 8.30pm that the baby was delivered at 4.24pm in the exclusive Lindo wing at St Mary's hospital, Paddington, west London. His name will be announced in due course. 'We could not be happier,' the Duke of Cambridge said.

In a statement, Kensington Palace said: 'Her royal highness the Duchess of Cambridge was safely delivered of a son at 4.24pm. The baby weighs 8lbs 6oz. The Duke of Cambridge was present for the birth. The duchess, who had planned for a natural birth, experienced at least 10-and-a-half hours labour, which Kensington Palace said had 'progressed as normal'.

'The Queen, the Duke of Edinburgh, the Prince of Wales, the Duchess of Cornwall, Prince Harry and members of both families have been informed and are delighted with the news. Her royal highness and her child are both doing well and will remain in hospital overnight.'

☑ Progress Check

Swap your live blog with a partner. Read through their blog and feedback. Swap again. How effective do you feel your blog is?

IT'S A BOY

9 Digital Generations

↻ Objective

Explore the ways in which different generations use technology to enable communication.

As technology advances, each generation has to adapt to new methods of communication. Read the newspaper article that begins on page 153 to explore how three generations of the same family stay in touch.

'Even if you are not necessarily thinking exactly what you might mean, you are making a choice about choosing a particular word over one that means pretty much the same but has got a slightly different meaning. I think that is why people are interested in language, because we have to use it in order to make ourselves understood.'

Fiona McPherson

✎ Activities

1 Identify the main methods of communication used by each generation of this family and summarize their views about these.

2 Timothy Pallett says 'I wouldn't put anything online that I believe to be secret.' Discuss whether or not you agree with this statement.

3 Miranda Hamilton says 'Texts blend conversation with written communication.' Explain what she means by this.

4 What difficulties does Chloe Hamilton find with modern methods of communication? Do you recognize any of these in the way teenagers today use modern technology to communicate?

5 Interview other members of the class to find out:

- the main methods of communication they and other teenagers they know use
- their views on the positives and negatives of each of these
- how they think communications technology affects the way teenagers use language.

THE DIGITAL ETIQUETTE GENERATION GAME: IS TEXTING RUDE? IS VOICEMAIL FOR DINOSAURS? AND HOW SHOULD YOU SIGN OFF AN EMAIL?

Timothy Pallett, 76, grandfather

'I wouldn't put anything online that I believe to be secret'

There are things you get from a letter which you can't get from an email. In my desk I have the last letter my first wife, Chloe's grandma, sent to me. I've kept it all these years and I'll never chuck it away. I recognise her handwriting as though I received it this morning. That familiarity is lost in an email.

I use the telephone to arrange to meet my chums. If I want to talk to someone, the first thing I'd do is ring them. Failing that, I'd send them an email. I might do that writing on the telephone thing, but to be honest, I rarely send texts.

It amazes me when people send me a text but don't answer when I phone back. They've had the phone in their hand not two minutes before. But usually I phone my chums, they answer and that's about the strength of it.

I'm not quite sure how to do a personal communication on Facebook, but I think I've done it before. I usually just read other people's entries instead. I've never tweeted in my life, I don't even know if I have Twitter. My mum always said, 'Never write anything down you wouldn't mind the whole world reading.' I think exactly the same about Facebook. I wouldn't put anything online that I believe to be secret. It applies to voicemail too. I wouldn't record anything which I wouldn't mind the whole world hearing.

I use my iPad for emails, and this FaceTime thing is great. I just put Miranda's email address in and job done. I live in Spain for half the year, so the iPad means we can talk to family while we are out there. It's terrific!

When I was at university, my friends and I would phone each other up (using a telephone box was commonplace), make arrangements and then stick to them. There are so many forms of communication now. I think this means people make last minute plans, or they make arrangements which they simply don't keep.

'Never write anything down you wouldn't want the whole world reading'

More to explore

Miranda Hamilton, 51, mother

'Texts blend conversation with written communication'

My mother wrote letters to me every week when I was at university, which I loved. She liked writing as well. Although I enjoy writing to Chloe almost every day on Facebook, the pleasure of receiving letters has been lost along the way, which is a shame. A thank-you letter is the only reason to send a letter nowadays.

I like writing, so sending Chloe a Facebook message gives me a chance to reflect on what I want to say. I am able to incorporate everything into a piece of text without being interrupted. When we talk together, be it on the phone or in person, we all talk over one another. It's easier if I write it all down. Texts and Facebook messages are an on-going conversation, rather than written communication. In a way, they have the formality of spoken interaction, with the **semiotics** of written language. We're blending these two forms of communication.

Whenever I see an interesting update on Chloe's Facebook profile, I'll think, 'Wow that's brilliant!' and I'll text or phone her. But I'm aware my friendship with her on Facebook is a privilege, not a right. I know at the press of a button she could de-friend me.

Before the days of Facebook my friends and I would send each other letters. Gradually we all signed up to Facebook, except one. But Facebook can be a force for good. I was recently reunited with a long lost friend on Facebook. We met when we were 15 and exchanged letters for years before life took over and we lost contact. A year ago, she found me on Facebook and our friendship was re-kindled.

Good communication is wholly dependent on how reliable the other person is. Chloe is always only a text away. My father, however, often doesn't have his phone on him, so the best way to contact him is to call his landline.

📖 Glossary

semiotics   the study of signs and symbols

> Wow Chloe! I just read what you got on Facebook. I'm ever so proud of you! Lots of love. Mum X

Chloe Hamilton, 22, daughter

'It's unusual for me to use my phone to call someone'

I'm a child of the digital age, so social media has seeped into every nook and cranny of my life. I can access Facebook, Twitter and both my email accounts from my iPhone, and with the Facebook phone app I can update at the bar, on the bus, or in the office.

But social media is so demanding. While it's comforting to know wherever I go I'll be kept **abreast** of my friend's relationship status or videos of her cats, I can't help thinking I'd manage fine without this information.

I decided to 'log off' for two weeks last summer and, believe it or not, the world kept spinning. Instead of checking my Facebook page first thing in the morning, I could be showered, dressed, fed and watered, and ready to crack on with my day in under an hour.

It's unusual, however, for me to use my phone actually to call someone. The only person I call regularly is my mum. We can chat for hours. So rarely do I ring anyone other than my mum that I once ended a telephone interview with 'Love you lots. Bye.' I'm also guilty of not sending letters. The tradition of thank you notes died out with my childhood. I received a love letter once, which was very exciting but never repeated.

If I want to talk to my Granddad I'll call his landline. He doesn't pick up Facebook messages, although occasionally he'll surprise me with an email.

Email sign-offs trip me up. I can deliberate for ages over whether to end an email with 'best wishes' or 'kind regards', because I don't know how formal an email should be. I once, accidentally, signed off an email to a university tutor with 'xxx'. Now I stick to 'thanks' or 'cheers'.

I like the brevity of Twitter, and it's good practice for a journalist to have an online presence. But it's not a reliable method of communication.

📖 Glossary

abreast   up to date

🕐 Extra Time

Interview different members of your own family to find out how they use technology to communicate, and their views about this.

10 Assessment: Giving a Presentation about Language and Technology

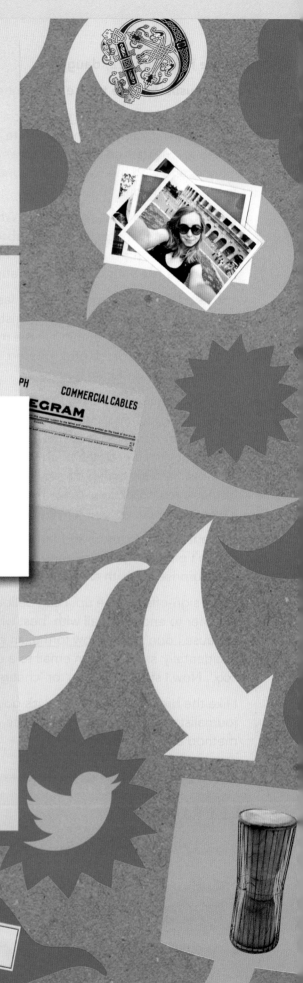

Your school has been asked to contribute to a national debate on how teenagers use and are affected by communications technology such as mobile phones, Twitter, Facebook, etc. Your Head Teacher has asked you to present your thoughts and views on this issue to your class. Here is the notice your Head Teacher has sent:

> I am particularly interested in hearing about:
> - the different types of communications technology teenagers use and why
> - how different types of communications technology affect the way teenagers read and write
> - how you think communications technology has changed the language you use, e.g. using new vocabulary, etc.

Using the skills and knowledge you have developed throughout this unit and the research you have conducted, you are going to present your thoughts and views on this to your class.

You will need to:

- communicate information and ideas clearly

- speak clearly and fluently, selecting an appropriate tone, pace and intonation.

Note that you are being tested on your spoken English skills, rather than your writing skills in this assessment.

Before you present…

Plan: Make a list of the different types of communications technology teenagers use. Think about the effects each has on the way teenagers read and write and the language they use. Make notes and begin to organize your ideas.

Plan the structure of your talk or presentation. Try to incorporate any research you have conducted and think about how you can draw on your own experiences to support the points you make. You could use visual aids and other resources to inform and interest your audience.

As you present…

Focus: Speak clearly and confidently, using expression in your voice to emphasize the key points you want to make. Keep your eyes on your audience, using voice and body language to keep their interest. Stay focused and keep to the structure of your presentation. Remember, if you are using visual aids or other resources, refer to these at the right time.

KS3 National Curriculum and *Ignite English* mapping: **Reading**

National Curriculum: subject content	Unit 1: Dare to Scare	Unit 2: Relationships	Unit 3: Exploring Difference	Unit 4: My Life, My Choices	Unit 5: Young Entrepreneurs	Unit 6: From Talking Drums to Tweets
Develop an appreciation and love of reading and read increasingly challenging material independently						
Reading a wide range of fiction and non-fiction, including in particular whole books, short stories, poems and plays with a wide coverage of genres, historical periods, forms and authors. The range will include high-quality works from:		L3	L2, L3, L4	L2, L3, L4, L5, L6, L7, L8, L9	L1, L3, L4, L5, L8, L9	L1, L3, L4, L6, L7 L8, L9
• English literature, both pre-1914 and contemporary, including prose, poetry and drama	L1, L2, L3, L4, L5, L6, L8, L9	L1, L2, L3, L4, L5, L6, L7, L8, L9	L6, L7, L8			L5
• Shakespeare (two plays)	L7			L4 (TC)		
• seminal world literature			L5			
Choosing and reading books independently for challenge, interest and enjoyment	L9					
Re-reading books encountered earlier to increase familiarity with them and provide a basis for making comparisons						
Understand increasingly challenging texts						
Learning new vocabulary, relating it explicitly to known vocabulary and understanding it with the help of context and dictionaries	L3, L5 (TC)	L3	L7 (TC)	L5, L7, L8	L1, L3, L5	L5, L6
Making inferences and referring to evidence in the text	L3, L4, L5	L1, L2, L4, L6, L7	L5, L6, L7, L8	L9	L1	
Knowing the purpose, audience for and context of the writing and drawing on this knowledge to support comprehension	L7 (TC)	L4 (TC), L6, L9	L2, L7 (TC)	L4, L7, L9	L4, L5 (TC), L8	L5, L8
Checking their understanding to make sure that what they have read makes sense	L3, L4, L5	L2, L4, L5, L9	L6, L7	L1, L6	L3, L8, L9	L1, L4, L5, L6, L9
Read critically						
Knowing how language, including figurative language, vocabulary choice, grammar, text structure and organizational features, presents meaning	L1, L2, L3, L4, L5, L6, L8, L9	L1, L5, L7, L8	L2, L3, L4, L5, L6, L7, L8	L2, L3, L4, L5, L7, L8, L9	L9	L5, L8
Recognizing a range of poetic conventions and understanding how these have been used	L5	L1, L2, L6, L7	L6			
Studying setting, plot and characterization, and the effects of these	L1, L2, L3, L4, L5, L6, L9	L5, L8	L3, L6, L7, L8			
Understanding how the work of dramatists is communicated effectively through performance and how alternative staging allows for different interpretations of a play	L7					
Making critical comparisons across texts	L4, L6 (TC), L7 (TC), L9	L1 (TC), L2 (TC), L4 (TC), L9	L6			L6
Studying a range of authors, including at least two authors in depth each year	L1, L2, L3, L4, L9	L1, L2, L3, L4, L5, L6, L7, L8, L9	L5, L6, L7			L5

Key: L = Lesson (Student Book); TC = Teacher Companion

KS3 National Curriculum and *Ignite English* mapping: **Writing**

	National Curriculum: subject content	Unit 1: Dare to Scare	Unit 2: Relationships	Unit 3: Exploring Difference	Unit 4: My Life, My Choices	Unit 5: Young Entrepreneurs	Unit 6: From Talking Drums to Tweets
Write accurately, fluently, effectively and at length for pleasure and information	Writing for a wide range of purposes and audiences, including: • well-structured formal expository and narrative essays	L9		L8			
	• stories, scripts, poetry and other imaginative writing	L1 (TC), L4 (TC), L5 (TC), L6, L8	L3 (TC), L6, L7, L9 (TC), L10	L3, L5, L6 (TC), L7 (TC)	L4		
	• notes and polished scripts for talks and presentations			L4 (TC), L6	L4	L6, L9	
	• a range of other narrative and non-narrative texts, including arguments, and personal and formal letters		L3 (TC), L8	L4, L6 (TC)	L2, L3, L5, L6, L8, L9, L10	L4, L6	L1 (TC), L2, L3, L7, L8
	Summarizing and organizing material, and supporting ideas and arguments with any necessary factual detail	L5	L1	L2 (TC)	L1 (TC), L3 (TC), L7	L1, L6	L4, L9
	Applying their growing knowledge of vocabulary, grammar and text structure to their writing and selecting the appropriate form	L1 (TC), L6, L8	L6, L10	L4, L5, L6 (TC)	L3, L4, L6, L8, L9, L10	L4, L5, L9	L3, L4, L8
	Drawing on knowledge of literary and rhetorical devices from their reading and listening to enhance the impact of their writing	L6, L8	L6, L10	L3, L4, L6 (TC)			
Plan, draft, edit and proofread	Considering how their writing reflects the audiences and purposes for which it was intended	L6	L6, L10	L4	L2, L6, L10	L4, L6	L4
	Amending the vocabulary, grammar and structure of their writing to improve its coherence and overall effectiveness	L6	L6, L10	L4	L2, L6, L10	L4, L6, L9	L4
	Paying attention to accurate grammar, punctuation and spelling; applying the spelling patterns and rules set out in English Appendix 1 to the Key Stage 1 and 2 programmes of study for English	L6	L6 (TC), L10		L2, L10	L4, L9	

Key: L = Lesson (Student Book); TC = Teacher Companion

KS3 National Curriculum and *Ignite English* mapping: **Grammar and vocabulary**

National Curriculum: subject content	Unit 1: Dare to Scare	Unit 2: Relationships	Unit 3: Exploring Difference	Unit 4: My Life, My Choices	Unit 5: Young Entrepreneurs	Unit 6: From Talking Drums to Tweets
Extending and applying the grammatical knowledge set out in English Appendix 2 to the Key Stage 1 and 2 programmes of study to analyse more challenging texts	L2, L3, L4, L8	L5	L3, L7, L8	L2 (TC), L8, L9		L3
Studying the effectiveness and impact of the grammatical features of the texts they read	L2, L3, L4, L8		L3, L7, L8	L8, L9		
Drawing on new vocabulary and grammatical constructions from their reading and listening, and using these consciously in their writing and speech to achieve particular effects	L8		L3	L1, L8, L9	L9	L3, L8
Knowing and understanding the differences between spoken and written language, including differences associated with formal and informal registers, and between Standard English and other varieties of English	L8 (TC)	L5			L4, L9	L3, L7
Using Standard English confidently in their own writing and speech			L8	L1, L8	L4, L9	L2
Discussing reading, writing and spoken language with precise and confident use of linguistic and literary terminology	L2, L4, L8	L1, L5	L3, L7, L8		L4	L3, L7

Also available: A wealth of SPAG interactives on Kerboodle LRA 1, 2 and 3.

KS3 National Curriculum and *Ignite English* mapping: **Spoken English**

National Curriculum: subject content	Unit 1: Dare to Scare	Unit 2: Relationships	Unit 3: Exploring Difference	Unit 4: My Life, My Choices	Unit 5: Young Entrepreneurs	Unit 6: From Talking Drums to Tweets
Using Standard English confidently in a range of formal and informal contexts, including classroom discussion		L9	L1, L4 (TC), L5, L7 (TC)	L1	L2, L3	L1, L2, L5, L7, L8, L9
Giving short speeches and presentations, expressing their own ideas and keeping to the point			L1, L6	L1	L7, L10	L9
Participating in formal debates and structured discussions, summarizing and/or building on what has been said	L1 (TC), L5 (TC), L6 (TC)	L3	L1	L3 (TC)	L2, L3	
Improvising, rehearsing and performing play scripts and poetry in order to generate language and discuss language use and meaning, using role and intonation, tone, volume, mood, silence, stillness and action to add impact	L1 (TC), L3 (TC), L7	L2, L4	L6			

Key: L = Lesson (Student Book); TC = Teacher Companion